Praying Like a Woman

Nicola Slee

First published in Great Britain in 2004 by
Society for Promoting Christian Knowledge
Holy Trinity Church
Marylebone Road
London NW1 4DU

British Library Cataloguing-in-Publication Data
A catalogue record for this book is available from the British Library

ISBN 0-281-05599-8

10 9 8 7 6 5 4 3 2 1

Designed and typeset by Kenneth Burnley, Wirral, Cheshire
Printed in Great Britain by Ashford Colour Press

Contents

For all who have prayed with me and for me.
For all who have helped me craft the words.
For all who keep the places of silence.
For all who enter the darkness.

Preface

Very many people have taught me how to pray, and most of them probably know (or knew) nothing about it. I learnt from an early age about faithful praying from my Devonian grandparents, Norman and Leafy Slee, who were farmers and staunch Methodists. My parents, too, passed on something elemental about the importance as well as the struggles of faith. Neither were given to talking much about religion, but they lived out faithfulness in their different ways. As a child, I enjoyed a special bond with my father when he took me to Sunday evening service at Providence chapel; we shared a companionable silence that didn't need to articulate what we were doing because we both knew it was important – and still do. My mother has taught me more than she knows about praying by her struggles to live truthfully and by daring to be different. Of my wider family, my Auntie Marjorie has upheld and supported me through the years with her steadfast and quiet prayer. All these deep family roots continue to nourish my life and faith.

As a young teenager I came into contact with two Methodist deaconesses, Sisters Marie Watson and Madeleine Swasey, whose vibrant faith had a profound impact upon me and brought me to a point of living commitment. The Reverend Kenneth Hext, my school chaplain, introduced me to the study of theology and demonstrated the possibility of combining devotion with a critical, scholarly understanding of the scriptures and religious faith. At Cambridge, my theological and intellectual horizons expanded hugely, but the heart of my life there for seven years was focused in the Chapel at Selwyn College, where the Master, Dean and Chaplain and members of the community kept the daily round of offices going. Along with generations of Selwyn alumni, I owe a particular debt of gratitude to John Sweet, not only for the theology he taught us, but also for the example of prayer he lived out, teaching us how to wait in silence upon the God who comes.

While at Cambridge, I first began to encounter and grapple seriously with feminist ideas and the feminist challenge to faith. Kirsten Baker played an important part in engaging and challenging me with new ideas about politics, gender and faith during one long summer working vacation on Dartmoor – and making it fun! I began to get involved in the Movement for the Ordination of Women and, later, Women in Theology. The sheer creative energy and sense of boundary-pushing of those networks is difficult to recapture in these days when feminist theology and liturgy are well established, but they were heady days and immensely important in forming a vision and a consciousness in many of us, both women and men. We experimented with different forms of liturgy and ways of doing theology, and I learnt what it means to pray and think with passion, with anger, with the body, with the senses. Much of what follows in these pages owes an obvious debt to those networks and the women who formed them.

Later, in London, I was part of the experimental St Hilda Community and a more local liturgy group which met at St Mark's, Wimbledon (we never gave ourselves a name). During this time I met Peter Kettle, with whom I shared many conversations about liturgy and a number of creative liturgical projects. A shared Triduum with some dozen friends at Micklepage is a particularly memorable occasion when we made our own liturgy from scratch, drawing on the experience of the group and responding to the context and the moment. More of that happened on the Southwark Ordination Course and the Aston Training Scheme, both of which provided wonderfully creative and liberating contexts in which to work out theology and authentic prayer in a community of adult learners. I particularly value the friendship, conversations and shared prayer of my colleagues Martin Baddeley and Alan Race from SOC, and Roger Spiller, Peter Hammersley, Patricia Fletcher-Kaye, Chrissie Whitehouse and Debbie Browning from Aston – not to mention the wider team of part-time Aston colleagues with whom I have shared some amazing conversations and encounters. Since 1997 I have been based at the Queen's Foundation, Birmingham, and once again feel immensely privileged to work in a theological community where, week by week, liturgy and prayer are created and celebrated with great creativity, energy and a willingness to experiment. I have learnt a great deal from students and staff with whom I have shared the ongoing pattern of prayer and worship – so many that it feels invidious to single any out.

Theological colleges and courses are places of intense transitoriness, by their very nature: most students are only part of the community for two or three years, staff may not stay for much longer and every year the whole community undergoes radical change. One has to look elsewhere for stability. For me, St Mary's Abbey, West Malling has provided that anchor of stability over a good number of years now. It is a place of extraordinary beauty, stillness and holding (though not without struggle and change) and the place itself, as well as those who live out a profound commitment to prayer there, have shaped my spirituality and my understanding of prayer in ways which go deeper than words. However infrequently I visit, simply knowing that it is there and that the sisters keep vigil night and day, sustains my life in a way for which I am deeply grateful. Many of the poems and prayers in this collection were written at the abbey in its huge, modern concrete church whose austerity somehow allows the prayer and the presence of God to take centre stage, or in the small, ancient pilgrim chapel nestling under the gatehouse. Since I moved to Birmingham, Glasshampton monastery has become a more accessible place of prayer and retreat which I have come to love and value. Nearer to home, the parish church of All Saints, Kings Heath has welcomed me gladly and, though I fear my own commitment to it is haphazard, I nevertheless receive much from the way in which its clergy and people seek to live out a faith grounded in prayer and oriented to the world.

Friends of many convictions and practices have shaped my understanding of what it means to live and pray faithfully. Gavin D'Costa, Jo Jones, Kate Lees and Peter Kettle have all prayed with me and for me over many years and have stretched my own praying by their lives and by the demands as well as the joys of our connection. My godchildren, John Featherby, Nathalie Richards, Thomas Sudbury, Hannah Skinner and Morven Cameron, have pulled me into faithful praying simply by being. Nathalie, in particular, has challenged me to pray 'without ceasing' as I have grappled, with her and with her parents, with the inexplicable nature of an illness which has dogged her life since birth. Valeria Moore CSMV, Mary John Marshall OSB, Deirdre Burton, Ramona Kauth and Donald Eadie have each at various times offered me spiritual accompaniment and companionship out of the rich stores of their grace, wisdom and lived prayer.

A number of others have had a more direct impact on this book by reading parts or all of the manuscript and commenting upon it. I belong to two writing groups, and the members of each of them have commented, at various times, on a fair number of the pieces in this book. Their questions and insights, and the care they take over words and what lies beneath them, have informed my writing and also my praying. My deep thanks to David Hart, Peter Freeman, Judy Tweddle, Rosie Miles, Gavin D'Costa, Eleanor Nesbitt and Ruth Shelton. David Hart read the whole manuscript and was honest enough to confess his discomfort with it, partly because of his own location in relation to the Church, and possibly because, as a man, he could not identify with some of the pieces. He may not think I have taken much notice of his comments, but I have! Janet Morley, whose *All Desires Known* is, to my mind, *the* feminist liturgical text above all others against which any subsequent work has to be measured, offered me detailed and pertinent comments which enabled me to revise and improve the text, and a conversation when I was in despair about responding to my editor's suggestions! Ruth McCurry at SPCK has been a clear-sighted, firm and critical friend of the book, believing in it from the start but holding me to the revisions I needed to make and waiting patiently for the finished manuscript. Donald Eadie, a wise and trusted spiritual companion, read the manuscript and helped me to reflect on the significance of its coming into print in my own life's journey. Rosie Miles, my partner and closest friend, also happens to be a fine poet and literary critic and, though she might dispute it, a woman of spirited faith. She not only read the manuscript and made many helpful comments, but also encouraged me through the stops and starts of this project with her unshakeable belief in me, her capacity to make me laugh, and her constancy. Her love, along with that of so many others, has midwifed this book into being. Snowy the Buddhist cat sat on the manuscript, purred at me whether it had gone well or badly, and reminds me that it is not only humans who may enter into, and reflect, the depths of divine grace.

NICOLA SLEE
Stirchley

Chapter 1

Praying Like a Woman

We must pray with eyes wide open, refusing to see nothing of what is hidden, secret – blatant lies.

We must pray with heads held high, refusing to bow in obsequiousness to prelate, priest or pope.

We must pray with tongues loosened, ready to cry out our anger, rage, pain and desire, refusing any longer to be silent.

We must pray with bodies known, bared: touching our own knowledge, knowing our instinctual wisdom, refusing to be violated or shamed.

We must denounce false ways of praying, false names for God, false myths and images and stories.

We must accuse our God of all that has abused us, crippled us, maimed us. We must drag deity to court, testify against him, lay the charge at his feet, bring forward many witnesses and see what he will answer. We must refuse all excuses, justifications, legitimations. We must insist on the charge, 'Guilty'.

We must lament our lost history, liturgy, story. We must bewail our betrayed bodies, knowledge, beauty. We must reproach our abandoned altars, mourn our overturned tables, weep for the broken vessels: the sacred chalice shattered, scattered in a thousand pieces.

We must search out the sacred sites, covered over with centuries' layers of forgetfulness, dust of denial. We must dig down deep into the earth of the past, retrieve what can be salvaged, report what our excavations uncover:

Item: a broken gold lacquered bangle, intricately patterned with hieroglyphs no longer decipherable, a language untranslatable.

Item: a woman's shoe, tiny and distorted; layer on layer of binding that kept the wearer's whole body restrained, teetering on the edges of freedom but only able to gaze over.

Item: a thin strand of dried bronzed hair, tied in a knot, carefully placed in a small leather pouch. Origin of specimen: female, unknown age and condition. Identity of the wearer: uncertain. Purpose and meaning of the custom: unknown.

We must carry on our excavations, urgently, painstakingly, dredging up the memories, knowledge, artefacts. We must piece together the assembled understandings: sort, arrange, rearrange, unscramble, dismember, remember. We must consult with one another about our findings. We must question, hypothesize, challenge, reconceptualize. We must ask the unaskable, speak the unsayable, chart the unnavigable.

We must talk together, endlessly, unhurrying, and without censure, ridicule or limitation. We must gather around tables, campfires, lecture halls, sickbeds, gravesides. We must lubricate conversation with liquor, laughter, levity. We must carry on long after the last child has fallen asleep, long after the menfolk have all gone home.

We must keep each other company in silence. We must cherish the good silences of wonder, completion, ecstasy and intimacy. We must wait out the heavy silences of uncertainty, ambiguity and anguish. We must come against the deadly silences of paralysis, passivity, hatred and abuse. We must learn all the many languages of silence, discriminate between them, know when to tarry, terminate or tease our way out of wordlessness.

We must find a way of knowing and of praying which is ours. We must test each inherited tradition, each learnt discipline, each accepted way. We must learn to say 'No' in many different tongues: tartly, fiercely, tearfully, proudly. And when they will not hear us, we must repeat the one word again and again, firm, unrepentant, immovable:

No. No. No.

We must know our 'No's as intimately as our own bodies, the lines on our faces, the slant of our shoulders, the strength in our hands. We must know what holds us back from uttering our refusal, we must push against the blockages, we must help each other move the stones.

We must stand sentry outside our re-opened graves, ready to meet whatever angel will appear there. We must hurry to where the tombs are being opened, the dead reawoken. We must go with spices, fragrant oils, arms full of flowers. We must call to our own dead, standing at the edge of the darkness, peering into the fecund shadows, feeling the warm air moving where for centuries there was only stillness.

We must open our own graves, like Spencer, and help each other clamber out. Each one, pull one. Some are naked, casting about for clothing. Some may be maimed or wounded, searching the garden for a healing. Some pick up exactly where they left off, before burial: bickering and hollering, undressing, dreamily sniffing flowers or smoothing down a son's collar, ironing the crisp cotton of a daughter's frock. It's our garden, we can grow it as we please. We must become our own gardeners, waking the land, working it so that it will yield the harvest we've been hungry for longer than we can remember.

We must dive down into the wreck, dredging up what has been silted over for centuries. We must salvage what we can, going down again and again, into the murky depths. Who knows if we will find gold untarnished or treasures rusted over, ruined and useless? Perhaps we will find perfectly preserved artefacts, untouched by salt or brine. Like the bog bodies, thousands of years old, preserved pristine in mud, the wrinkles on the cheek exquisitely patterned, the hairs on the chin each one countable, the trusting demeanour of the resting heads and closed eyes for all the world akin to the attitude of our own sleeping child's. Just so miraculously, perhaps odd memories and traditions may have escaped the ravages of tide and time, locked in some air-sealed container deep in the earth, perfectly formed, gift from Before.

This is what we must do, what some of us have been doing, what we'll carry on doing for a long time to come: working the territory, weaving the tapestry, making the journey. Learning a new language to sing and stutter and shout all we've been aching to say all our lives. And finding how to do it as we do it, learning as we practise, making the way as we walk it. Following no blueprint, copying no precursor, we'll craft a journey unpredictable, cast a pattern asymmetrical and intricate, as delicate as it is unrepeatable, tender and indestructible, made of colours vivid, tenacious, wild.

*   *   *

This is something of what it means to me to 'pray like a woman'. Put more prosaically, it means to live into the experience of being a woman, in the particular time and place in which I find myself, before the face of others and of God, with as much intentionality, attention and awareness as I can muster. Such a definition begs many questions, both about what it means to be a (white, Western, middle-class) woman at the start of the third millennium, about what it means to pray 'before the face of others and of God' and about the nature and identity of this God before whom one prays. I don't attempt to answer these questions in this text – at least, not directly, not in prose terms – because it is not that kind of book. It is a book born out of the process of trying to live and pray as a woman over some twenty or more years, and anything I might have to say about that process is reflected in the poems and prayers themselves.

The process of 'praying like a woman' is one which has engaged struggle, anger, lament, exhaustion, contemplation, waiting, wondering, discovery, delight, passion, sensuality, sexuality, politics and theology, both shared and solitary, not necessarily in that order and not necessarily in any order at all. Nevertheless, some kind of journey into voice and into the reality of praying and living as a woman seems evident to me, as I look back over the past twenty years or so. The chapters which follow chart something of that journey. It is not necessary to read the book consecutively, from cover to cover, and I guess most readers will not do so. But for those who do, it may help to say a few words about the unfolding sequence of that journey.

This chapter, consisting largely of the prose poem, 'Praying like a woman', can be read as a condensed summary of the whole book, in one sense. This piece which I wrote a few years ago for no particular audience or occasion other than my own need to write it, expresses in miniature something of the larger journey from resistance, struggle and anger through to celebration and resurrection which is then engaged on a larger canvas in the rest of the book. Reading this chapter, then, provides – I hope – something of an overall context and orientation for all that follows. Chapter 2 engages the struggle against paralysis and pain which has been a marked feature of my journey into voice and selfhood as a woman, wrestling against the many forces, overt and covert, which have attempted to silence me. This struggle has resulted in much sorrow and regret for the wasted time and opportunities that mark my life, as well as for the thousands and millions of women, both in the present and in the past, who have never made it into voice or whose stories have got lost along the way. Sorrow and lament therefore form a major substance of this chapter.

Chapter 3 is a reclaiming and articulation of the liberating and healing effects of anger, defiance and rage. Anger has not been perceived as a womanly virtue nor as a Christian one, yet feminists and liberationists more generally invite women to recognize and channel their anger as a powerful force for good. Sorrow and anger are different reactions to the reality of oppression and struggle that mark a woman's journey into selfhood. I want also to speak of a different experience of silence, darkness and unknowing, not as forms of oppression, but as strange and mysterious gifts into awareness of life as gift and grace; this forms the substance of Chapter 4.

Chapter 5, perhaps the pivotal chapter of the collection, celebrates the coming into voice, the daring to declare of a woman who has wrestled with her anger, sorrow and paralysis, waited out the darkness of unknowing and entered, finally, into speech. The pieces in this chapter speak out of reclaimed authority and conviction, and, at their best, contain a self-authenticating energy and veracity. Chapter 6 concerns a connected but different kind of reclaiming: the reclaiming of women's memory, history and past. Many of the pieces in this chapter are retellings of women's stories from the Bible and Christian tradition, the overlooked women standing in the shadows, such as the prodigal's mother or the prostitute in the story who is mentioned only in passing and in scathing tones by the elder brother. These are women who, until the past few decades, have been consigned to silence and whose stories and voices are only now being recovered.

While the whole of the book exemplifies, I hope, an embodied consciousness, a writing out of the body and the senses as much as the mind and reason, Chapter 7 reflects in a particular and self-conscious way on what it means to be female in a woman's body, and on some of the particular experiences of *this* woman's body – menstruation, hysterectomy, childlessness. Throughout the book, too, there is a profound consciousness of the interconnectedness with others which is a central feature of feminist spirituality. Chapter 8 celebrates the 'many kinds of awesome love' which have been important in my life, both those that are widely recognized, such as the love of family and partner, and those that are not, such as the love of friends and the love that is born out of solitude or the labour of work. Chapter 9 is a sensual, passionate affirmation of joy, celebration and praise, an outpouring of the goodness and wonder of being a woman fully alive, not in spite of, but in and through the struggle against the forces that would crush that life. Finally, Chapter 10 reflects self-consciously on what it might mean as a woman to name and approach 'the edge of God', and offers a variety of images and narratives by which to approach that mystery.

As I have already made clear, the pieces in this collection represent something of my journey and experience over a twenty-year span. Hence they do not necessarily represent a unity of perception or experience. Some were written out of singleness and solitariness, others out of a profound sense of connection and partnership; some were occasioned by illness, struggle and apparent sterility; others issue from times when life was flourishing and fecund. Some pieces are highly personal, intended only for personal use; others were written specifically for a particular group or community and are intended for wider communal use. I think the nature of the piece, its appropriate audience and the range of its use will generally be clear. The notes at the end of the book give further details about the original context of composition, where appropriate, and, if previously published, the original source. For those wanting to use the book for public liturgy and worship, there is a liturgical index to aid ease of access to relevant material in the book. Likewise, a biblical index indicates where material relating to biblical texts may be found.

I have entitled this book *Praying Like a Woman* because the material emerges very directly and specifically from my own particular embodied experience as a woman of a certain age living in a certain context and speaking from a certain vantage point. I am conscious that I am one very particular woman, hence it is 'praying like *a* woman' rather than 'praying like *women*' in general or in the abstract. I hope that women very different from me as well as men will read this book, not necessarily to identify with the particularities of its context and the occasions which sparked its contents, but in order to be encouraged and inspired to pray more deeply and authentically themselves. My hope is that whoever picks up this book may be encouraged, in their very different contexts and out of their very different experiences, to pray as and who they are, towards who they may yet become.

Chapter 2

Motherless Children Weeping in the World Alone

Sorrow, paralysis, pain

Suffering has been a dangerous subject for the disempowered, including women. For not only have women collectively suffered acutely at the hands of men, but Christianity as a religious tradition has legitimized the oppression and victimization of women (as of slaves, children, black people, lesbians and gays) through its language and symbols of suffering. In particular, the ethic of sacrificial suffering, writ large in the symbol of the crucified Christ, has been used as a means of reinforcing women's passivity, powerlessness and pain. Women have been encouraged to put up with their lot in silence and suffer with and for Christ. Feminists have rightly protested against this pernicious use of the image of the dying and suffering Christ, and there has been a struggle to resist and overcome suffering in the name of a God who desires fullness of life for all.

Yet suffering and pain remain a reality of daily experience – if not one's own, then certainly others' – with which religious faith has to do. There is the sorrow of illness, of physical pain and diminishment with which most of us have, at some stage, to do. Although I have never experienced profound physical pain, I have been plagued with minor ailments of one sort or another for most of my life and explore the challenges of sickness in a number of the following pieces. There is also the sorrow of loss and bereavement: the dyings and woundings of many kinds that we endure by dint of living and loving and changing. There is, too, a particular kind of struggle against paralysis, against powerlessness and passivity, against voicelessness, with which the disempowered have to engage. In my own life there has been an ongoing struggle against inertia and enfeeblement that has been a striking part of my journey as a woman into voice and into selfhood. The sins which cling so tightly (Hebrews

12.1) and against which I have had to struggle and cry out for the mercy of God are not so much those age-old vices of pride and aggression that male theologians have decried as the besetting human sins, as the sins of torpor, weakness, lack of belief in my powers, dividedness, the fear that keeps me stuck in places of paralysis, the half-aliveness of timid living; or, conversely, the over-extension of self into too many projects and directions that saps my body of energy and drains the imagination of its drive.

The pieces in this chapter speak, in different voices, of my struggle with woundedness, with sorrow, with loss, with powerlessness, with sickness and stuckness. These pieces employ at points the language of lament and reproach, those age-old biblical forms in which human sorrow and pain are brought before God and catalogued, narrated, wailed and keened in the divine presence, in the insistence that God must hear, God must know the suffering of God's people and that, hearing and knowing, God must act. Lament gives expression to the profoundest experiences of dislocation and lostness, isolation and pain, brings them before God in prayer and protest and insists on a divine response to disorientation and pain.

Sorrow

that my lover will one day leave me
that no one can love me for ever
that my baby will never be born
that when I am seen for all that I am
I will be rejected

that this love of mine must struggle to be spoken
against the voices that say it is forbidden
that this love of mine must push against so much
to come into the open

that my life is faithless
and endlessly falling away from itself
into its own nothingness

that I come from a people of brokenness
and there is no end to the breaking

that the well of sorrow is deep
and its depths shall never be sounded

that hurt is at the heart of things
and cannot be undone

that we are all motherless children
weeping in the world alone

that sorrow is never done
that sorrow is never done

No one told you

After a car accident

no one told you
what it would be like
to live in the aftermath

how your head
would keep on shaking
with the reverberations
for months

how your stomach
would churn and churn
throw up bile
green and foul-smelling

how your muscles
would ache
raw and tender
at gentle human touch

and bunch themselves
in hard knots
that constricted
your every movement

no one told you
how the body stores
the memory of shock
along with the mind

how a word or a look
can start the shaking again

how the pores
release the poison slowly
and won't be hurried

and you must cry often
and go into the pain
and you must submit
to the hammer blows
that split your head
and the lurchings
that unseat your stomach

and you must lie quiet and spent
for days afterwards
without motion
without intention

and you must hold yourself
tenderly

because no one told you
until today

Morning sickness

I wake feeling sick.
I drag myself out of the warm cocoon
of the brushed cotton sheets
into the already late sunlight of morning.

I wake into sickness.
I wake into the knowledge that I am useless.
My body is heavy and listless.
She will not work for me today.

It will pass, it will pass.
Soon I will be able to drink coffee.
Soon the smell of frying bacon
will not turn my stomach over.
One day, one magic morning over the horizon,
I will wake into sunlight
and the rays will not hurt my eyes
and I will leap up
into the morning
and I will be ravenous
and I will be laughing
and the tiny seed inside me will be stirring
and I will be imagining
what she will look like
what I will name her
how she will grow like me
or not like me.

But for now
I wake into nagging nausea.
I drag myself into the bloated morning.
There is no cure save birthing.

For all the sick ones

For all the sick ones
For all the stuck ones
For all the down-on-their-luck ones   *mercy*

For the paralysed
For the terrified
For the mortified   *mercy*

For those who can't finish
For those who won't fulfil their promise
For the ones who never got started   *mercy*

For the ones stuck in their cells
For the ones stuck in their beds
For the ones stuck in their heads   *mercy*

For all the ravers
For all the mourners
For all the demented   *mercy*

For the bleeding
For the pleading
For the unheeding   *mercy*

For our lack of madness
For our unfeeling sadness
For our soul's paralysis   *mercy*

For all the sick ones

Lament for a lost friendship

O my sister, my sister,
  what wrong have I done to you?
What good have I not done for you?
  Turn again to me and listen to my words.

Once we were close companions, barely to be parted.
Our lives ran together like the waters that flow as one into the
    ocean.
But now our rivers have diverted, flowing separately to the sea.

O my sister, my bride, you were all that was sweet to me.
Like honey in the hive, your words nourished me.
Your company was to me more than the tenderness of lovers.
Your embrace to me was sweeter than the union of mother and
    child.
In the shade of your branches I rested and found shelter.
In the fragrance of your garden I walked and happiness came to
    meet me.

But now the hive lies open and the honeycomb is dry,
the vine has withered and all its grapes have soured.
The leaves of the tree are scattered and its branches bare,
the garden gate is locked and you have thrown aside the key.

O my sister, my sister,
  what wrong have I done to you?
What good have I not done for you?
  Turn again to me and listen to my words.

Search me and try my thoughts that you may know me,
question me that you may judge me and acquit me.
If there be any evil in my heart, show me and I will wipe it clean.
If there be any lying on my tongue, accuse me and I will cut it out.
If I have offended against you, speak to me so that I may answer.
If I have wounded you, tell me, so that I may heal the sore.

My heart cries out in anguish when I think of you, O my sister.
My eyes fill with tears when I lie on my bed at night and
     remember you,
  O my equal, my companion, my friend.
If I forget you, my beloved, let my right hand wither.
Let my tongue cleave to the roof of my mouth, if I do not
     remember you,
if I do not set your friendship above my highest joy.

O my love, in the clefts of the rock, in the covert of the cliff,
let me see your face, let me hear your voice.
Hide not your face from me in the day of my trouble.
Turn to me again, and I shall live.

O my sister, my sister,
  what wrong have I done to you?
What good have I not done for you?
  Turn again to me and listen to my words.

Let us go again to the house of our God, where our feet once
     walked with gladness.
Let us go again to the city of God's people, arm in arm rejoicing in
     God's love.
Remember again, my dear one, the companionship of former days.
Call to mind all that we once shared in the days of our youth.

Have mercy on me, my sister, have mercy upon me,
for I have had more than enough of contempt.
My soul has had more than its fill of suffering,
my eyes more than their fill of tears.

To you I lift up my eyes, O you so far from me.
As the eyes of a maid look to the hand of her mistress,
so I look to you, beseeching you to have mercy,
    waiting until you turn and show kindness to me.

O my sister, my sister,
  what wrong have I done to you?
What good have I not done for you?
  Turn again to me and I shall live.

Collects

Luke 19.1–10

Christ whose piercing gaze sees all that I have been,
all that I am and all that I can be:
forgive me for those I have wronged,
for the time I have wasted,
for the living I have squandered.
Show me how to turn my life around
so that I can face you and others more truly
and enter into that freedom
for which you tell me I am made.

Psalm 22

Absent yet present God,
in the well of our sorrows, teach us how to sing the blues,
in the terrors of desolation, give us a voice to sing the blues,
in the anguish of isolation, enable us to keep on singing the blues,
in the starkness of all suffering, give us an ear to hear your blues,
and, in the midst, to catch a glimpse of the presence of the Singer.

Psalm 23

God of all comfort and strength,
soothe us when we are hurt;
calm us when we are afraid;
hold us when we are alone;
support us when we are tired;
lead us through the valley of the shadow
to the place where we can, at last, come home.

Prayer to Mary

John 19.25–7

When we stand in the place of death and loss,
    Mary, stand with us,
    and teach us how to endure.

When we stand in the place of powerlessness, unable to act,
    Mary, stand with us,
    and teach us how to hold fast.

When we stand in the place of separation,
    Mary, stand with us,
    and teach us how to let go,
    releasing ourselves and all for whom we yearn
    into the mystery of divine love,
    so that we may become ready to move on
    into the new community of love where God's Spirit calls.

Eucharist for World AIDS Day

The gathering

Today we are gathering.
We are gathering as a broken body.

We are the maimed and the wounded.
We have marred your image, glorious, in us.
We bear in our fractured bodies the pockmarks of our sin.
We are bleeding, we are suppurating.
The pus runs from our scars and will not be stopped.
The stench of our brokenness is palpable.

Lord have mercy,
Christ have mercy,
Lord have mercy,

On the body politic that does not hold,
On the bodies of the babies dying in Africa,
On the bodies of the addicts craving and desperate,
On the bodies of young gay men grown suddenly old,
On the bodies of the sleek and rich who think themselves
     immune,
On the body of the earth, scarred and maimed,
On the body of the Church, broken and divided.

Lord, have mercy on us all.

Today we are gathering.
We are gathering around the broken body.

Christ, though resplendent in beauty,
yet for our sake you became sin.
Though you had the lover's dazzling countenance,
you took upon your flesh our fallenness and frailty.
You bared your back for our protection.
You bore the lash for our healing.
You endured the sores for our well-being.

You bled so that we might cease our bloodshed.
You were pierced so that we might be whole.

Look upon our infirmities with compassion.
Gather the wounded into your arms.
Lift up the afflicted to the throne of glory.
Bear the broken little ones who have none to carry them.
Tend the dying sick ones whose time has come.
Watch over the grieving grandparents, mothers, fathers, sisters,
    brothers, partners and friends.

Lord, have mercy on us all.

Prayers of intercession

Today we are gathering.
We are gathering for the broken body.

We do not come alone.
We weep with the stricken communities of Africa.
We lament with the child sex workers of Calcutta.
We come into the light with the hidden HIV victims of Asia.
We stagger with the junkies of Chicago and Edinburgh.
We bring in our arms the sons and daughters of bank managers
    from Harlow.
We dance with the hordes streaming out of Soho's nightclubs.

In every yearning body a heart beating for love.
In every broken body a mind hungry for thought.
In every living body hands needing to serve.

Silent or spoken prayers are offered.

Ministry of the sacrament

Today we are gathering.
We are gathering to give thanks for the broken body.

We lift these hands before you in honour, worship and praise.
We adore you for the love which has held us from our birth and
    will hold us until our death.

We implore you for the healing of your broken body, the earth.
We intercede for the broken bodies of all the diseased and
    distressed.
We rejoice in every work of justice that brings your shalom into
    the world.
We offer you our selves to be taken, blessed, broken and given,
as you yourself were given for us.

On the night on which you were betrayed,
you gathered your friends together
to share the last meal before your death.
You took bread, gave blessing, broke the loaf and said:
'This is my body, which is for you. Do this to remember me.'
And the cup, too, you offered to them, saying:
'This cup is the new covenant in my blood.
Do this, whenever you drink it, to remember me.'

Come then, Holy Spirit of God,
Stand with all who fall.
Raise the dying. Restore the hurting.
And breathe into this cup and bread the healing for which we
    long.
As we eat, may our broken bodies be renewed.
As we drink, may the wounded earth be redeemed.

O God, we adore you in your broken body!
O Christ, we adore you in your shed blood!
O Spirit, we adore you in your life poured out for all!
Alleluia! Alleluia! Amen!

The invitation

The body of Christ broken for the world's healing.
The blood of Christ shed for the world's renewing.

The bread and wine are shared.

Post-communion prayer

As we have shared in the broken body,
so may we share Christ's compassion.
As we have been nourished by the broken body,
so may we nourish others in our own brokenness.
As we have glimpsed God's longing for healing,
so may our lives now be gladly spent in the service of that dream.
Amen.

A canticle of suffering

You shall endure storms of chaos and floods of destruction,
    while all that you once knew is perished,
so that I may bear you up upon the waters
    and bring you into a world of which you have not dreamed.

You shall be driven into the wilderness,
    enduring aimless wanderings and futile disputations,
so that I may feed you with manna
    and speak tenderly to your heart.

For my thoughts are not your thoughts,
nor are your ways my ways, says your God.

You shall be sold into captivity,
    becoming slaves to cruel captors and exiles to your own land,
so that I may strengthen your weakened resistance
    and teach you to sing my song in a foreign land.

You shall know fire, pillage, war and devastation,
    escaping only with your very life,
so that I may become all in all to you
    and carry you unharmed through the flames.

For my thoughts are not your thoughts,
nor are your ways my ways, says your God.

You shall be counselled falsely by erring teachers
    and lulled into complacency by false prophets
so that I may instruct your heart secretly
    and teach you to discern my ways.

You shall be divided from mother and father,
    and sister and brother shall betray you
so that I may embrace you tenderly
    and comfort you in my arms.

For my thoughts are not your thoughts,
nor are your ways my ways, says your God.

You shall doubt my providence and despair of your calling,
    fearing divine displeasure and delusion,
so that I may be with you even in absence
    and teach your heart to trust even when it fails.

You shall be taken out far beyond your strength and your
        understanding,
    and, after enduring for a time and a season,
you shall endure and endure again,
    so that I may become the God of your salvation
and perfect my glory in your flesh and your frailty.

For my thoughts are not your thoughts,
nor are your ways my ways, says your God.

Sower

For the ending of the Aston Training Scheme

Here at the open gate
go on again:
nothing shall be the same.
All that is sown now lost
at unmeasured cost,
the prodigal seed
scattered by warm wind
and quickly gone from view.
But where no eye can see
the hard dry husk may fall,
penetrate the moistness of soil
and, after lying waste,
expunged and erased,
root in dark earth,
shoot up in some unimagined field,
sprouting amongst grain or weed
where unknown others walk
through an open gate
to gather, harvest and feed.

Sower, go on.

Chapter 3

Storming the Silence

Anger, defiance, rage

Marge Piercy has a poem entitled 'A just anger' in which she portrays anger as a potential force for good, a transfiguring energy that lights the path towards justice, something 'beautiful as lightning' and 'swift with power'. It has taken me half my life to be able to feel my anger, let alone express it in ways that are healthy and healing and contribute to the common good. I, like many women, grew up somehow imbibing the message from my schooling, from my reading and from my church attendance that good girls didn't get angry, nice women didn't feel rage and that, if I wanted to be loved or accepted, I'd better act sweet and loving and kind. Anger was something permitted in boys and men, but in girls and women it was fearful, ugly, absolutely unfeminine. The Church is not good with anger. So often its representatives don't seem to know how to express collective rage or respond to the personal and social anger of others. Our liturgies, for the most part, hold no place for railing and raging against God, even though the scriptures contain many examples of the saints and prophets doing precisely that.

The claiming of our anger as a cleansing, healing, cauterizing, liberating and transfiguring force with potential for good is a major step on many women's journey towards claiming their selfhood and voice and power. And there is plenty for women to be angry about: injustice in all its forms and guises; poverty; the hypocrisy and complacency of the Church and of society's institutions; violence against women, children, the elderly and weak, animals and other species; the ravaging and despoliation of the earth. The list could go on. Women's anger needs to be owned, expressed, heeded and acted upon. If it is suppressed and swallowed, its potential to do harm is only intensified. Anger turned inwards upon the self becomes paralysis and depression or is translated into bodily sickness and pain.

This chapter contains expressions of anger, rage, denunciation, protest and reproaches of different kinds. Some are flung in the face of God, others are aimed at the Church, others again at individuals who have acted unjustly or betrayed trust. Others deal with the struggle to allow one's rage to come to voice and expression. Standing in the ancient tradition of protest and reproach, they rework this tradition in new ways to give voice to women's rage and fury: a rage that, given appropriate expression, can, I believe, be a beautiful power for good in the Church and the world.

Psalm of anger

St Mary's Abbey, West Malling

Rage ricochets off the empty cloister walls,
anger erupts at the altar.
The silence palls.
My serene piety falters and crumbles.
My lips mouth the prayers
but my heart lurches and stumbles
on the edge of this gaping pit
into which my cries have fallen.

I will storm this silence
not with praise but with venom.
I will blast this emptiness
not with patience but with anger.
My mantra is not 'mercy'
but a cacophony of curses
hurled headlong at your distance,
spat in the face of your absence.

Show yourself!
Answer me!

I am sick of your silence,
I have had my fill of your hiddenness,
I am faint with the worry of waiting
on your word which never comes.
Have you not seen my pain?
Have you not heard
the anguish of my heart?
How can you stand far off
and watch me writhing and straining for you
with my bleary, tear-filled eyes,
crying for you with my dry and weary throat?

Why do you gloat from afar?
Will you not come?
Will you not show yourself?
Answer me!

Speaking of silence: a reproach

The sounds of women's silence run deep.
Let us attune our ears to the sounds of women's silence,
to attend and listen to what is not said,
what has never been said,
what is only now beginning to be said.
Let this silence cry aloud in our ears,
let it resound and reverberate inside our heads,
let it deafen our whole being with its colossal roar.

This silence is eloquent, articulate of women's pain and women's
   lives.
It is compelling, hypnotic, fearful, overwhelming.
It speaks louder than words.
It utters volumes of speech.
It drowns out all other language.

Where are the women in our history, in our heritage?
Where are the stories of our women heroes, mystics, leaders and
   teachers?
Who will guide the footsteps of our daughters
born today into a deafening silence about their ancestors, about
   themselves?

So many women's voices have been lost in the pages of history,
erased and blotted out and passed over in silence
by the rulers of patriarchy, the makers of culture.
So few have survived in the pages,
and their stories have so often been ignored,
trivialized, marginalized, distorted.

We want to hear the sounds of our foremothers' voices.
We want to listen to our grandmothers' tales.
We want to speak the names of our sisters who came before us.
We need to hear their stories,
we need to hear their voices,
to hear and know who we are.

Women's silence: a confession

O women, whose voices have never been heard:
we repent of our deafness,
we confess our stubborn hearts and closed minds.

O women, whose words have been consigned to silence:
we grieve for the wisdom which has been lost.

O women, whose wisdom has not been heeded:
we desire that our time will be different and
we commit ourselves now to listen.

We will turn again to search out the scriptures.
We will look for the clues of your lives in the margins of history's
    pages.
We will seek out your words in secret places.
We will dig for your treasure hidden deep in the dark.

For we know our need of your wisdom.
We yearn for the restoration of what has been lost.
Our time is hungry for your forgotten stories,
for the ancient art of women's wisdom
which will heal our hurt and may yet save our world.

Letter to the Church

Dear brother Church:
I name you 'brother' not 'mother',
for your leaders are mostly men
and your ways are still too patriarchal.

I want to live passionately.
I will not hide my anger or my energy.
Will you face your own?

I want to act effectively.
I will not deny nor dissemble my power.
Will you admit your own and be willing to share it?

I want to think dangerously.
I will not set limits on what it is possible to ask or say or explore.
Will you open the gates of learning you have been guarding and
    let others in?

I want to pray deeply.
I will not withhold any part of my life from the divine gaze.
Will you plunge with me into the depths?

I will work with you,
but I will not work for you.

I will walk with you,
but I will not lead you nor will I follow in your path.

I will weep with you and laugh with you,
but I will not feel for you;
you must claim your own passion and pleasure and tears.

I will offer you the fullness of my being,
but I will not sacrifice myself on the altar of your impossible
    demands.

Dear brother Church,
I am standing here as a woman struggling to be who I am.
I am speaking:
are you listening?

The fathers

The fathers are losing their power to harm us.
See, the long line of daddies falling like ninepins.

One was a banker:
his stocks and shares are shrunk.
One was a farmer:
his land has been razed.
This one was a lawyer:
someone stole the key to his ledger.
That one was a priest:
his altars lie abandoned.

Where do they go, the daddies,
when they start to keel over?

If we're not very careful,
they will creep into our bellies,
taking up residence in the soft, fleshy hollows
where our blood will keep them warm.

We hear their weedy little voices
magnified by the walls of our stomachs:
'O daughters dear! Be careful!
Be watchful! Do not harm us with too much truth!'

We have to tell them, 'Fathers, dearests,
it's time for you to lie down now.
It's time for you to roll over.
Your day is done.'

Knock them over and they bounce back again.
You have to get out your gun and shoot them,
looking them straight in the eyes
and telling them you love them,
O you've never loved them better,
than the day you aim the trigger,
aim the trigger and pull.

Mary Magdalene: a liturgy of denunciation and reclamation

'Anyone who loves the biblical Mary Magdalene, and compares her with the "Christian" Mary Magdalene, must get very angry.'
(Elisabeth Moltmann-Wendel)

Magdalene, we are angered by the lies
they have told about you;
Magdalene, we are angered by the truths
they have concealed about you;
Magdalene, we are angered by the power
they have robbed from you.
We claim our anger,
We vent our anger,
We choose to use our anger
to denounce, to renounce, to reclaim.

We denounce the hateful names they called you:
Prostitute, Whore, Harlot;
Temptress, Sinner, Slut.
Delectable Detriment, Smouldering Seductress, Rampant
   Repentant.
Mad Woman, Crazed, Crazy:
Out of her mind,
Out of her head,
Out of her brain.

We renounce the pernicious images they painted of you:
voluptuous, sensuous, curvaceous,
every straight man's best sexual fantasy.
Your hair is always long and loose,
cascading down your body in delicious abandon,
sign of your looseness, availability.
Or they made you half-starved and anorexic,
giving you the wasted body of the madwoman
suggesting self-neglect and abuse.

We denounce the lies,
We renounce the myths,
We reclaim your story anew.

They painted you grovelling at the feet of Jesus,
never tall and upright, meeting him face to face.
You must be lowly and abased,
wallowing in your worthlessness.
We see you crouched under the supper table,
pouring out your ointment on Jesus' feet
and using your hair to wipe them clean.
Or swooning and swaying beneath the cross
barely able to stand upright,
out of your mind in your agony and grief.

We denounce the lies,
We renounce the myths,
We reclaim your story anew.

We see you speechless and silent –
you! the one who proclaimed the resurrection! –
sitting in rapt contemplation at the feet of Jesus,
eagerly devouring his every word without a single question, query
   or murmur
to disturb those who do not wish to hear
what you might have to say.

Even in the garden you always seem to be kneeling,
stooping and gesturing towards the Lord's body,
reaching for his feet yet again.
Jesus towers above you,
gracious but condescending,
as if to have you standing upright
would somehow compromise his authority.

We denounce the lies,
We renounce the myths,
We reclaim your story anew.

We reclaim the names with which
they should have honoured you:
Woman of noble stature,
woman of upright life,
woman of bold countenance and bearing.

Woman of means, woman of substance,
providing out of your largesse for Jesus and his companions.

Magdalene, we honour you.

Healed woman,
woman released from oppressive forces,
woman set free from all that would imprison or limit or
    straighten.
Free woman, refusing to be contained
by the strictures of men
or the bondages of patriarchy.
Unowned, your own person,
self-possessed, self-defining, self-giving.

Magdalene, we salute you.

Woman with a mission,
commissioned by Jesus to go forth and tell.
Woman of the strong voice, the powerful witness, the
    acknowledged authority.
Woman of courage,
woman of boldness,
woman of purpose,
whose voice unleashed the Easter story.

Magdalene, we revere you.
We stand tall in the shadow of your stature,
We speak boldly with the courage of your voice,
We claim our power in the tradition of your own.
We denounce the lies
We renounce the myths
We reclaim your story anew.

Texts of terror

For the reading of difficult scriptural texts

There are ancient texts in the scriptures that, for centuries, have
been used to terrorize and victimize women. These texts show
women as victims of abuse, hatred and violence. They depict
women raped, murdered, dismembered, abandoned, betrayed, sold
into slavery, maltreated, silenced, subjugated. They do not cry out
against women's misery, abuse and pain. They do not whisper a
word to suggest such deeds are wicked, evil, shameful. They do not
denounce the God who demands such acts to be done in his
name.

These texts speak terror, yet we seek healing.
These texts cry misery, yet we are looking for mercy.
These texts magnify violence, yet we are praying for gentleness.
These texts justify oppression, yet we are working for liberation.
These texts make us shudder.
These texts make us angry.
These texts cause us to weep and to wail and to lament
our own and our sisters' pain.

These are the texts of terror.
These are the texts that have taunted and terrorized us.
These are the texts that have silenced us and savaged us.
These are the texts over which we have
wrestled, ranted, wept and raged.

Should we remember Hagar, Tamar, Jephthah's daughter and
    Lot's?
Should we tell of their wretched lives to our daughters?
Should we speak on our lips the tales of torture, misery, abuse and
    violence?
Would we do better to consign them to silence?

We will listen, however painful the hearing,
for still there are women the world over
  being raped
  being whipped

being sold into slavery
being shamed
being silenced
being beaten
being broken
treated as worthless
treated as refuse.

Until there is not one last woman remaining
who is a victim of violence

We will listen and we will remember.
We will rehearse the stories and we will renounce them.
We will weep and we will work for the coming of the time
when not one baby will be abandoned because of her gender
not one girl will be used against her will for another's pleasure
not one young woman will be denied the chance of an education
not one mother will be forced to abandon her child
not one woman will have to sell her body
not one crone will be cast off by her people and left to die alone.

Listen, then, in sorrow.
Listen in anger.
Listen to the texts of terror.
And let us commit ourselves to working for a world
in which such deeds may never happen again.

Veneration of the cross

I cannot venerate the glorification of unnecessary suffering,
but I can venerate all those who work to alleviate suffering
and bring its causes to judgement.

I cannot venerate violence and victimization,
but I can venerate the forces of life
that resist the forces of death and destruction.

I cannot venerate the cross as somehow uniquely sacred,
but I can venerate all who die with dignity, courage and trust
and name them each as holy, God-bearing, grace-filled persons.

As I take the cross in my hands and kiss it,
I am committing myself,
not to sacrificial suffering, but to the struggle for life
which nevertheless has to wrestle
with the forces of death and destruction and hostility.
I am saying I am willing to be engaged in that struggle and to pay
    its cost.

I am choosing life with open eyes,
I am cognisant of the cost such a choice may demand.
I am aligning myself with all who work for justice, peace and
    liberation.
I am placing myself on the side of life.

Christ whose cross has been used and abused
to justify slavery, the abuse of women, the misery of the poor:
Make us strong to resist every exploitation of another
and ready to pay the cost of the struggle for life.

Prayer for friends turned enemy

Perhaps I could pray for enemies,
it would be straightforward.
They would be the ones who hate me,
who wish to do me harm.

But these: these are the ones I thought were friends.
These are the ones I have eaten with
and prayed with and laughed with.
These are the ones
with whom I sat at Christ's table.

Now, without warning, they have turned from me.
They have wounded me in the deepest place of my vulnerability.
They do not speak to me, they will not look at me.

I do not know how to pray for them.
I cannot pray with them.
I have only rage and anger and pain and confusion to bear them.

God, you alone are faithful.
Accept the prayer I cannot make.

What have we done?

What have we done that you cannot welcome us?
What is our crime that you do not acknowledge us?
What sin have we committed that you will not speak to us?
What horror do we bear that you will not look on us?

Our only crime was to love our own kind.
Our only sin was to demand equity.
Our only misdeed was to declare our love openly.
Our only dishonour was to hold up our heads shamelessly.

O you that judge all hearts, judge between us.
O you that welcome sinners, welcome the spurned.
O you that were among the rejected, stand with those who have
    been rejected.
O you who know all secrets, let what is hidden be disclosed.

Chapter 4

Under the Brooding Breast

Silence, darkness, unknowing

There is a kind of darkness and a form of silence that are character-
istic of the night of faith when one walks by trust and intuition
rather than knowledge or sight. There is the darkness of night, of
rest, of cessation of activity, the darkness of abandonment into the
fearful yet merciful love of God who is beyond naming, beyond
imagination, beyond grasp. There is the contemplative silence of
wordless waiting upon God and with God: not for any particular
thing, but simply to be present, with as much attention as one can
muster, in the presence of the One who is mystery, otherness, grace
and source of all that is.

The poems and prayers in this section are concerned with
darkness, silence and unknowing. Some of them were written out of
a time when much that was good and wholesome in my life seemed
to be pared away: I was made redundant and the community which
had been to me my people was disbanded and closed down; I
became ill with Chronic Fatigue Syndrome and had to give up my
own home and lodge with others; I had to have a hysterectomy,
forcing me to confront my childlessness; the farm which had been
in my family for three generations was sold and the family home
lost. In all this time, I had the sense of much that had been familiar,
known and trusted being stripped away, and of being carried out
beyond my understanding into some new place or reality of which
I could only dream. I knew I could only go forward; the way back-
wards was closed for ever. The biblical narrative of the flood came
to mean much to me during this time, and a number of the pieces
which follow are written around this narrative. Other pieces were
written out of more stable periods of life: during times of retreat
and withdrawal, often at Malling Abbey, and often during the
winter months when darkness was in the ascendancy. What they all

share is a sense that darkness, winter, silence and unknowing are necessary counterbalances to the pull of light, summer, speech and knowledge, those activities of the rational, conscious mind and of the will. Not only that they are necessary counterbalances, but that they may admit one into the heart of gospel truth in a particular, graced way. For in the silence of contemplative prayer, in the darkness of faith stripped down to the bone and in the unknowing that is the other side of the illusion of control, I may learn that I do not own my life but that it is gift, that I am worth more than all my achievements or failures, and that I am not saved through any thing I may do, make or know, but by the unconditional, incommensurate love of God.

Dark

Malling Abbey Church

Here in the dark
do not speak.
      Only
listen, hold your peace
and wait for the wordless gift:
the lifting of the lark's voice,
choice and sweet,
repeating its high note of love,
speaking your name,
calling you over and over
again.
  Do not speak.
Let the visiting bird,
silence, do her work:
sift your heart,
heal what is broken,
sundered apart,
restore what is plundered,
repair the rift,
knit to one piece the unravelled mind,
scattered and split.

Wait for the gift,
the lifting of the warm,
beating wings,
the sudden shelter
under the brooding breast.
You must enter
here in the dark
where the heart sings.
Do not speak.

In praise of

the empty cup
the word unspoken
the dream that escapes me in the morning

the wasted day
the whole day in bed with my lover
sleeping snoring dreaming
the day when we forgot to get up

the extravagant sleep
the exhausted body
consenting to its own exhaustion

the vastness of ocean deeps unfathomable
the night sky unseeable
the unconscious where the mind cannot go
yet is forever returning

this is a poem
in praise of

the great dark that surrounds us
the vast 'O' that beckons us
the fearsome awe that threatens us

the places we can't go
the faces we don't know

the labyrinthine paths
the mind's mineshafts
the descent to the deeps
the abyss we don't reach

this is a poem
in praise of

what you don't know
where you won't go

Hole

After the Tao Teh Ching, *saying number 11*

keeping the hole
where it should be
so that the spokes
don't buckle

keeping nothing
right there
at the centre
preserving the tension

keeping what is not
in place
so that what is
may not displace it

keeping the O
round and yawning
and empty
refusing to fill it

letting the heart lurch
and the body quiver
and the tongue stumble
on its own hopelessness

letting the throat
constrict in wordlessness

letting the formlessness be

permitting the unmaking
of thoughts and lines and words
and the grasp of and the hold on things
over and over to slip

permitting the unmaking of soul

ah this keeps the doctors running
and the poets writing
and the singers silent
and the madwomen for long hours staring

Edge

Come into the deep
where the ocean floor
shelves steeply away
under the thrust of your feet.
Swim out
beyond your depth.
Plunge into waters
cold and sweet.

Come into the free,
cross the boundaries
of home or foreign place,
out into open space
where earth and heaven meet
and the land recedes
beyond your sight.
Taste the wide air,
sharp and sweet.

Come over the edge,
where the rocky ledge
gives way to vastness,
sudden stark. Dive
into wild air, wide time,
beyond your sense.
Freefall into space,
sheer and sweet.

This is the leap
into life and death
way out beyond
all sense and sight and depth,
where the empty air
and water and abyss
call
     Come.

No straight road

It's not a straight road,
though it is narrow.
From here to there,
to where you want to get to,
is no straight road.
And where you want to get to
may not be where you are going.
There is elsewhere.

Wherever it is you are going
you cannot see the way,
not because there is not one,
but because it is dark and narrow
and it is never straight
so that the eye could see it.
You cannot even tell
if there is a path at all.
You can only trust it may be so
in moments when the trust is given.

In between there are long hours, nights and weeks
that take years to tremble through
when you are alone
in some godforsaken ditch
exhausted from the hours of sweating labour
trying to heave yourself out.
Which you must do,
you cannot simply lie there and give up.
It is only when you do give up,
lying there bruised and icy cold and cut all over,
tears streaming down your whole body,
the heart of you utterly shaken –
it is only then that some stranger rounds the corner
sees your plight
and stretches out an arm to lift you.

Not merely to lift you:
to touch you

to cradle you
to wrap you in
poultice of prayer
to clothe you
with blankets of compassion
to salve your smarting wounds
to bind the tears that won't stop flowing.
And then at last
to lift you
to carry you
where you can't carry yourself
to do every tiny goddamn thing
you can't do for yourself
for you.

And you – what must you do?
Nothing.
Nothing at all.
It's all your labouring
and scraping of hands and knees
and struggle to get out the ditch
that keeps you there most surely.
Only when you lie there
silent and helpless
all hope abandoned
never knowing if the stranger is coming
may you be lifted out
and carried round
the next dark corner
of the road you can't see
and know
will never be straight.

Journey

Gazing out at the dim, impossible horizon,
there was no way of knowing
how long or arduous the journey,
nor even where or how to begin.
Only the dawning consciousness
that much would have to be shed.

First, the farewell to shelter,
the familiar comfortable dwelling,
the walls whose smells and stains you knew,
the well-fingered patterns of fabric and furnishings,
the firmness of wood under your hand.
Then the departure from kin,
the distancing from voice and touch and glance
of those in whose gaze
your life had grown and been beheld:
the warmth and blessing of the mother's body,
the timbre and loving of the father's voice.

So much that was treasured
would have to be relinquished:
pleasure of friendship, artistry, comfort,
ease of accomplishment, achievement,
honoured accolades and prizes.
Many desirable futures would have to be discarded,
each in their turn tasted yet yielded to emptiness,
the willingness to be aborted.

Even the flesh would have to be pruned,
pared to a delicate yet enduring sensibility,
a body lacking language,
wanting conception,
forfeiting strength and mobility,
compressed to a small bub of vulnerability,
ready to be thrown into life
      and death
           again and again.

Only after so much contraction
would the god be ready to begin.

Driftwood

Aldeburgh, Good Friday

How many times have they been under,
these sodden fragments of flotsam
pulled down by the tow,
thrust up again,
spat out on the shoreline?

Do they carry any memory
of the green leaf,
the strong root,
birdsong in branches?

Dark they are and mangled by numerous winters;
yet still I trace the mould of bark and bole,
and each holds its own grain,
coarse or fine,
weathered clean,
purged by tides.

Wrestler

Genesis 32.22–32

This, this is the place.
Seek love here where
love is displaced,
overcome by fear. Dare

to look again. Face
the stark wall
that blocks out all space.
Welcome dark. Fall

to fear that gives you chase.
Clasp your foe, hold
him in fierce embrace,
nor let him go. Fold

him to your chastened,
beaten heart. Wrest
the blessing from his graceless
lips. At once depart, lest

he should mark the face
turned to receive his gaze. Go,
hasten from the place.
The wound will always show.

A litany of waiting

Genesis 6—9

The first waiting was a time of working:
of measuring and sawing,
of hammering and of heaving;
while the people mocked
and there was no sign of rain.

The second waiting was a time of devastation:
of flood and storm and tempest,
of terror and of destruction;
while the earth was laid to waste
and not one creature was left alive.

The third waiting was a time of suspension:
of floating and being carried,
blown by winds and immense waters;
while the known world was perished
and no new land had come into sight.

The fourth waiting was a time of abating:
of restraint and of cessation,
of silence and withdrawal;
while the waters of the flood subsided
and the ark came at last to rest.

The fifth waiting was a time of testing:
of casting the bread upon the waters,
of searching and of scanning the horizons;
while the dove roved the earth
and found no place to rest.

The sixth waiting was a time of impossible patience:
of biding the time yet one more time,
of curbing the impatience and holding on for the final readiness;
while the bird returned with the sign of life in its beak
and in our hearts we knew the time for departure was at hand.

Prayer from the ark

Genesis 6—9

God of the floods and the tempests,
you call me into your ark
for a time and a season,
while you wreak havoc and destruction,
laying waste and bringing to naught:

Hold me fast in your ark,
while the floods rage
and the waters of chaos roar,
while all living flesh is destroyed
and the former things are made no more.

Keep me resting in your ark
while the rains are restrained
and the windows of heaven are closed;
while the waters recede upon the earth
and the sound of the floods is no more.

Keep me waiting in your ark
while the dove searches for a place to rest on the earth,
returns and waits and is sent forth again,
returns once more with the olive leaf in her beak,
and is sent and returns no more.

God of the rainbow and the clouds,
you bid me leave your ark
when the time has come
and my boat has settled on dry land:

Send me forth from your ark
while the world is made new
and your promise good;
to be fruitful and faithful upon earth,
to multiply your praise and your works
and to remember the former things no more.

Prayer for the waiting time

Give me the resolution to say 'No' to the good
so that I will be ready to give my 'Yes' to the better.

Give me the courage to keep living in the open-endedness of the
future
without foreclosing the mysterious work of your Spirit in my haste
or fear.

Give me the persistence to stay in the wilderness of unknowing
until I am ready to receive your call.

Give me the strength to keep still and waiting
when all about me is pushing towards movement and activity and
choice.

Give me the acceptance to live these days in uneventfulness,
simplicity and hiddenness,
without craving excitement, distraction or change.

Give me the grace to live in the emptiness of not doing
without the rewards of achievement, fulfilment or success.

Give me the wisdom to discriminate between my own impatience
to move forward
and your Spirit's deep stirring of my spirit when the time is right
to move.

Give me the faith to trust in your obscurity,
the obedience to stay faithful to your mystery,
the courage to keep tryst with your inscrutability.

Teach me

Teach me the art of gentleness,
to live patiently with my brokenness,
discern your presence in my emptiness.

Lend me a measure of faithfulness
to trust you with my helplessness,
to believe in a way out of hopelessness.

Show me the skill of carefulness
to guard the life in barrenness,
discover growth in separateness.

Lead me in your way of paradox:
confinement which effects liberation,
death birthing new creation.

Laying of the cloth: an Advent prayer

An empty crib or Moses basket is placed centrally in the worship space. Silence is kept.

This crib is the waiting space of our emptiness.
This crib is the waiting space of our loneliness.
This crib is the waiting space of our longing.
This crib is the waiting space of our hunger and our desire
                    for intimacy
                    for justice
                    for truth.

Come, O Christ-child
        into the cradle of our emptiness,
        into the crib of our loneliness,
        into the space of our longing,
        into the arms of our hunger,
        into the heart of our desire.

A cloth is placed in the empty crib.

We are waiting for you.
We are looking for you.
We are longing for you.
We are laying this cloth of our woven dreams and aspirations.
We are bringing the fabric of our lives:
        many-textured,
        multi-coloured,
        torn, frayed and fragile,
        yet tense with a strength woven out of conflict, laughter
            and tears.

Come, O Christ-child:
Clothe yourself with the cloth of our humanity.
Adorn yourself with the colours of our creatureliness.
Weave the cloth of your love and your longing for justice around
    us.
Wrap us in your vulnerability, compassion and tenderness.
Come and live among us,
and be present in the warp and woof of all our days.

The darkness of God: a blessing

For John Hull and Mike Holroyd

And the darkness of God will be to you a blessing
and the night shall become for you a path
And you shall walk in it with joy and gladness
and you shall run in it with head held high

And no marauding beast will assail you
and no unclean thing bar your way
For angels will guard you as you walk there
and guide you under the shadow of their wings

Until at last you reach the gate of hope
and go in under the doorway of delight
to be welcomed into the citadel of freedom
and to rest your soul under the portals of love

And there you shall be royally feasted
and seated in the banquet of love
And you shall hear your name called gently
and you shall enter into the darkness and gladness of God

And the blind shall lead you into God's dazzling darkness
and the deaf shall lead you into God's silent darkness
and the dumb shall lead you into God's eloquent darkness
and the lame shall lead you into God's dancing darkness

For in that city no lamp will shine
no sun or moon adorn the sky
For the darkness of God will lighten every sadness
and the splendour of divine darkness will dazzle every eye
And the fullness of divine glory will overshadow every longing
and the secret of divine beauty will satisfy every desire

And so the darkness of God shall be a blessing
and the shadow of God will be to you
a light more lovely than the dawn
a lamp more gleaming than the sun
And your blindness shall be the mark of your faithfulness
and God's faithfulness shall be sealed by the star of everlasting
  night

Chapter 5

Dare to Declare

Affirmation, conviction, commitment

For women, there is often a struggle to come to speech and voice, to be able to say, with confidence and conviction, 'This is what I know', 'This is my truth', 'This is so'. A woman may imbibe the sense from many quarters that she has no right to speak, no reality worth articulating, no authority to declaim – perhaps particularly in the religious realm where, for centuries, women have been enjoined to 'keep silence in the churches' (1 Corinthians 14.34). Yet when those who have been silenced, either through the social forces of oppression or their own internalized sense of worthlessness, begin to claim a voice, open their mouths and speak out, they often do so with a peculiar urgency and power, an authority that is born out of their struggle and anguish and pain. The knowledge they possess is deep, intuitive truth; the language they speak is passionate speech; the affirmations they make are authoritative utterance.

The pieces in this section concern the process of coming to speech, of finding a voice, and the content of conviction and commitment that have taken shape as I have claimed the right to articulate that which I know to be true. In some cases, this content of belief takes expression in recognizably traditional, if reworked, forms, such as the credal statement affirming what is believed about the nature and activity of God. In other cases, the affirmation of belief concerns subjects which have not been the focus of traditional doctrinal statements – affirmations about the goodness of the single life, for example, or the acknowledgement of my need of others.

Of course, the very process of writing anything at all is, in itself, a 'daring to declare', and the writing of poetry in particular may be a mysterious and liberating experience of discovering a truth one did not know one knew. It is not as if one sits down to write a poem with a preformed notion of what one will write or say. Poems frequently appear 'out of the blue' and what they know is often as much of a surprise to the poet as to anyone else. I often say 'My poems know more than I do', by which I suppose I mean my poems come out of a place of imaginative and intuitive knowing – the same place from which the knowing of dreams and art and contemplative prayer come – that is not amenable to more logical articulation or conscious control. It may take me years to live into the truth of my poems, if I ever do. Yet I have come to respect what they know and to trust in their veracity. Like all claims to knowledge, they must be tested against the bar of reason and submitted to the scrutiny of dialogue and debate. Most of all, they must be made true by being lived out in word and deed. Yet they may also have a self-authenticating ring, which others, as well as the self, can recognize in an answering 'Yes, I also know this to be true.'

Conversations with Muse

Dare to
declare
who you
are. It
isn't
far from
the shores
of silence
to the
boundaries
of speech.
The road
is not
long but
the way
is deep.
And you
must not
only
walk there,
you must
be prepared
to leap.

Nativity

St Mary's Abbey, West Malling

Something starts to shift, to move;
to prove I am not dead.
Something stirs inside my head.
The blood runs deep and red.
The pulse is firm and strong.
It will not be long
till she is born, till she is bled,
the life kicked sheer out of me
in one great tear, the flesh giving way
in its war against her own
unstoppable, unbiddable
    child.
        Child of my body,
she will emerge, bloodied but whole,
naked and tender as any newborn,
but fearless, resilient, perfectly formed.
        Child of my flesh,
she will thrash her vigorous limbs,
she will fill her young, never-tried lungs
thick with the fast approaching air.
And with one primeval scream,
she'll rend the void and utter her first
wordless, miraculous
                Word.

Open our lips

We have heard the sounds of women's silence.
We have listened to our sisters' voices.
We have been stirred by their passion,
encouraged by their strength,
instructed by their wisdom.

We, like them, wish to speak out.
We, like them, desire to speak truly.
We, like them, have a story to proclaim.
We long to midwife a new and living word for our time.

But often we are afraid.
We fear the sound of our own voices.
We would not know our own strength,
we would not claim our power.

We have no eloquence, no fine-sounding words or polished
    phrases.
Our speech is halting, we stumble and stutter over the words of
    life.
Our lips are sealed, like the tombs of the unliving.
Our tongues are heavy as stones within our mouths.

Come to us and speak to us in our weakness.
Set the fire of your speech in our throats,
and the burning coal of your passion on our tongues.
Loosen our lips to proclaim your praise.

O You, whose voice rolls over the waters
and thunders over the oceans,
whose word splits even the cedar trees
and breaks in pieces the cedars of Lebanon,

whose voice makes the oaks shake and shudder,
and strips the forest bare,
whose word whirls the sands of the desert
and resounds through the mountains:

Open our lips and our mouth shall declare your praise.

A single woman's manifesto

I want to be single
and not considered sexless,
frigid from the neck downwards,
lacking in passion and sensuality.

I want to be single
and not treated as dysfunctional,
pitied as unlovable, unchoosable, unhaveable.

I want to be single
and not rendered invisible,
ignored in restaurants,
passed over in advertisements,
relegated to the small print by travel agents.

I want to be single
and not regarded as infantile, incomplete or lacking in humanity,
'still searching' for the perfect partner,
'still waiting' for life to begin.

I want to be single
and not assumed instantly available,
able to drop whatever I'm doing
to respond to others' more pressing and immediate needs.

I want to be single
and not presumed timid, unadventurous or innocent,
having my hunger for life and for fullness diminished
by Church and society's narrowness.

I want to be single
and not have my needs considered insignificant,
assumed that I will be content with
hand-me-downs, second-hand bargains
and someone else's cast-offs.

I want to be single
and not have my friendships belittled,
considered less important than partnerships
or less committed than romantic relationships.

I want to be single
and have my capacity for parenthood recognized,
my need for nurturing and cherishing others validated,
my skills in caring and growing lives celebrated.

I want to be single
and not denied ritual, story and liturgy
to celebrate my choices and my struggles,
the milestones and the markers of my life's journey.

I want to be single
in a Church and a culture
which celebrates diversity and distinctiveness,
solidarity in difference,
friendship across otherness.

I want to be single.

A litany of prayer and praise for being single

For the pleasures of solitude
and for the pain of loneliness

For the freedom for many friendships
and for the fragility of those bonds

For the luxury of spaciousness
and for the privation of boundlessness

For the joys of independence
and for the burden of choice

For the intensity of the undiluted emotion
and for the anguish of the overwhelming feeling

For the clarity of single-mindedness
and for the uncertainty of going it alone

For the energy of freely chosen action
and for the exhaustion of carrying it through unaided

For the fruitfulness of imagination, mind and soul
and for the barrenness of body

For the delight of nurturing others
and for the distress when those connections are invisible, those
    ties unacknowledged

For the freedom from the constraints of coupling
and for the oppression of living in a society where coupledom
    rules

For the bliss and the bane of the single lot
its happiness and hurting
its ecstasy and anguish
its freedom and its fetters
its pleasures and privations

I yield my thanks
I make my pledge
I give my 'Yes'

With others: a statement of interdependence

I do not stand alone
but with others to support me
I will stand my ground.

I do not see the way
but with others to walk it with me
I can make a path.

I do not possess the truth
but with others to witness to what they know
I will be able to discern what is right.

I cannot master all skills
but with others who will lend their accomplishments
I can do enough.

I cannot carry every burden
but with others to share it
I may bear my own load.

I cannot meet all needs
but with others to nourish and replenish me
I will be able to give enough.

I do not have limitless free choice
but with others to consult
I will make my own choices gladly.

I will not always be consistent
but with others to laugh with me
I will regain my equanimity.

I am not invincible
but with others to reach out a hand
I may learn from my mistakes and start again.

I cannot be perfect
but with others to make up the shortfall of my imperfections
I can be content to be good enough.

Easter creed

We believe in God
  Maker, Redeemer and Sustainer of Life,
  without beginning or end,
  whose life-giving love was let loose on the first Easter Sunday
  and whose life-giving love we share and proclaim here today.

We believe in God
  who gave up the divine life and submitted to the darkness and
    terror of the grave
  and who enters with us into every darkness and terror we shall
    ever face.

We believe in God
  who raised Christ from the death of the grave to glorious new
    life
  and who raises our lives from sin and despair to newness and
    hope again.

We believe in God
  who met the grief-stricken Mary in the garden and called her
    into hope by the uttering of her name
  and who meets us in our grief and gives us courage to hope
    again by tenderly calling our name.

We believe in God
  who sent Mary from the garden to be the witness and apostle of
    the resurrection
  and who commissions us, like Mary, to be bearers of hope and
    good news in our world.

We believe in God
  Maker, Redeemer and Sustainer of Life,
  without beginning or end,
  whose life-giving love was let loose on the first Easter Sunday
  and whose life-giving love we share and proclaim here today
  to all women and men, wherever and whoever they are,
  loved, blessed and called by God,
  without beginning or end.

God of all time

Psalm 139

God of all time,
I believe that my past, present and future are in your hands.

God of all places,
I believe that there is nowhere I may go
where you are not there before me.

God of all life,
I believe that the vastest movements of the cosmos
and the most intimate thoughts of the human heart
are both of concern to you.

God of all experience,
I believe that the heights and depths of human aspiration and
    anguish
are known alike to you.

Help me to find my voice and to sing my song:
in the time that you have given me
in the places that I find myself
in the life that is mine to live.

Alpha and Omega canticle

Revelation 1.8

Alpha and Omega,
the beginning and the end;
in all our yesterdays, todays and tomorrows,
you are the One I Am.

You are older than all time,
younger than the newest born;
Ancient of ancients,
newborn from the wellspring of the world.

You meet us as Judge and Redeemer
of every botched beginning,
every aborted birth,
every fraught ending,
every untimely death.

You are present to renew and forgive
in every birth that seems like a death,
every death that surprises us with birth,
every enduring that appears unending,
every ending that seems to us unceasing.

You seek us out in generosity
in the generations of our passing,
in the ceaseless stream of time;
in the repetitions of human failing,
in the cycles of our search for meaning.

Come, Alpha and Omega,
Christ of all our times:
Breathe upon us your newness and your oldness,
your ancient and ageless blessing,
your youthful renewing presence.

Alpha and Omega,
the beginning and the end;
in all our yesterdays, todays and tomorrows,
you are the One I Am.

Field

Matthew 13.44

Within the heart there is a world
and in this world there lies a land
and in the land a certain field
and in this field is treasure hid

To search this heart and walk this world
to spy this land and find this field
to dig the loam and seize this prize

a merchant must hold nothing back
of land or love or world or goods
but ready to expend her all
she may at last the treasure glimpse

and there within the casket gold
see all of sundered wealth
and warmth and world and wilds
secured   made good

Chapter 6

Unfreezing the Frame

Remembering, re-reading, redeeming

It is not possible for me to claim my voice and authority as a woman alone. I need the company of other women to help me discover who I am, to help me speak out what I know. I need not only the company of other sisters in the here and now (though I certainly do need that); I need to know that I belong to a company of women of faith stretching back long before my own time and place: that I belong to a fellowship of women of wisdom, women who have also struggled to give expression, in their lives and in their words, to what they know to be true. I need women from the past – both alike and unlike me, from many different times and peoples and places – whose lives and struggles and achievements can instruct, inspire and nourish me. I need access to women's history, to *her*story.

Yet, as feminist historians, biblical scholars and theologians have amply demonstrated, women's history has been systematically repressed and excluded from the canon of recorded civilization as we know it. Feminists all over the globe are embarked on a mammoth quest of recovering, reclaiming, re-reading and reworking the texts and traditions of the past in order to unearth and celebrate women's lives, stories and contributions. There is anger and pain in this undertaking as well as joyous discovery, for, in the process of rewriting the past, we discover that so much of women's history has been irretrievably lost – and even that which has not been entirely lost has been so suppressed and marginalized that it has not been permitted to wield the influence it might have done. We are all the losers for this, but women in particular are deeply wounded by the loss of our collective history. For generations of women have been born into an overwhelming silence about their own past traditions, texts and ways of life, and this has perpetuated the lack of voice and confidence with which many women struggle.

The pieces in this chapter are all concerned with remembering and re-reading aspects of women's biblical and religious history, because this has been a vital part of my own coming into a sense of myself as a woman of faith standing in a tradition rich with the stories of other women's lives. A number of the pieces are reworkings of biblical stories from a woman's perspective, while others take a broader historical sweep. There is both celebration and mourning in these pieces, in roughly equal measure, but whatever their particular mood, the overall intention is to reclaim and redeem a past that rightfully belongs to all contemporary women of faith.

Unfreezing the frame

Luke 15.11–32

She is not there in the story,
though surely it was she who wept in the night,
anxiously turning in dream-disturbed sleepings,
conjuring the worst that could have happened
to her disappeared son.
And watching, uncertain whether to say anything,
the tight-lipped obedience of the elder son,
taking upon his narrow shoulders
the full weight of filial expectation.
And wasn't it she who comforted the father late at night,
when both lay unsleeping,
speaking hopeful futures
she longed, herself, to believe?

Surely she embraced the returning son
in arms as wide as the father's,
though Rembrandt has her only standing by,
almost swallowed up in the surrounding shadows.
I cannot believe her heart was any less broken
or, later, resurrected, than his.
And wasn't it she who stitched the seams of the robe
he ordered for the pitifully wasted body?

Yet the text remains closed to her grieving and her groping,
stubbornly refuses the breaking open of a mother's heart.
It's left to us, centuries later,
to prise open the fissures,
peer into the silences,
retrieve the waiting presences from the receding shadows,
usher the tongue-stopped women, startled, into the story,
displace the centre,
disrupt the tidily closed circle.

We'll call to all the wives, mothers, sisters,
harlots, orphans, gorgons, medusas,
mistresses, madwomen, militants, mutes and muses:

'Come out! come out!
Unstop your voices!
Open your mouths!
Speak the words you might have uttered
and never had the chance to say!'

We'll watch them all start up,
like figures in a frieze suddenly animated,
their frozen frames moving,
their limbs silently working,
their mouths opening and shutting as they gulp in the air,
try out their long-shuttered voices,
cry out their misery, antipathy, ambivalence, rage,
even their occasional joy.

Watch them spilling over the pages,
a stampede of women's feet
flattening the hills and prairies,
a cascade of women's voices
trilling and ululating over the sounds that have carried down to us
from the high places,
a swathe of women's bodies
moving through forbidden territory,
sweeping ancient pathways
clear of the dust and debris,
reconfiguring the continents.

And we're the ones who are to do it:
release the pause button
on history's long unrolling,
turn up the volume on the silent movies,
wind back the tape to replay the action,
watching for what was unnoticed, unremarked,
disappearing into the edges of the camera's viewpoint.
We're the ones, now, who'll unfreeze the frame.

A litany of women's voices

I am Eve. I argued with the snake and reached after wisdom.
For this I was banished from the garden.
Listen to me.

I am Miriam. I sang lustily
and led the women in praise of our God.
O hear me.

I am Deborah. I listened to my people's wrangles,
I weighed up evidence and judged between them.
Pay heed to the voice of my calling.

I am Ruth. I dared to declare my love of a woman
in words strong and true.
Let my cry come unto you.

I am Hannah. I wailed and begged and pleaded with the Almighty
for my child,
never heeding men's disapproval.
O hear me.

I am Esther. I kept cool in time of great danger
and used diplomacy and tact to save the life of my people.
Give ear to me.

I am Anna. I discerned the presence of great power
in a common Jewish baby
and gave utterance to God's praise in the Temple.
Listen to me.

I am the Syro-Phoenician woman, whose love for my daughter
drove me to Jesus.
I compelled his respect with my frank and daring words.
O hear me.

I am woman without a name,
yet my action of anointing Jesus spoke louder than words.
My story has been passed over in silence,

though Jesus said it should be remembered
wherever the gospel is proclaimed.
Pay heed to the voice of my calling.

I am Martha. I recognized Jesus and named him the Christ.
I believed in his power over death.
For this, I have been consigned to the kitchen.
Let my cry come unto you.

I am Magdalene. My only sin was sickness,
yet men have defiled my name.
I risked ridicule and relinquished the joy of discovering my
beloved.
I left the garden to go and proclaim the good news.
O hear me.

I am Mary. I gave my yes to God fiercely,
without reservation. I have kept my many thoughts
and secrets locked in the silence of my heart,
pondering them deeply,
while men set me on a pedestal and gazed at me from afar.
Give ear to me now.

We are the women who refused to keep silent.
We are the ones who claimed our power.
We named ourselves, we shaped our times,
we spoke the words of life.
We are the spokeswomen for the many who kept silent,
who, through fear, ignorance or brutal oppression,
never found their voices.
We are the guardians of the tradition of women's wisdom.
We are your mothers, your sisters, your friends.
Why, then, have you denied us?
Why have you refused our words?

Potiphar's wife

Genesis 39

I know what I want
I know who I want
and it's him
that young Israelite, Joseph

I coax him
I entice him
'Come, make love with me'

Not once, not twice
but day after day
seeking him
eyeing him
lusting after him

I'm the prototype of the lascivious woman
the poor little rich girl
who has everything she can ask for
but wants more

the teasing temptress
the sex-hungry seductress
the bored wife
the middle-aged woman
seeking a new diversion

History blamed me
long after he did

God, listen to his self-righteousness!
I loved the smell of power on him
the ease with which he'd risen to prominence
I loved his youthfulness
I loved his vigour
I loved his cocky certainty

Loved it and wanted to dent it
wanted to break into that self-assurance
wanted to see desire ripple its disturbing path over him
wanted to curb that energy
disrupt it displace it
cause a crisis in his manhood
bend all that goodness and vigour towards me
bring him into my orbit
bring him to his knees

Will you say you blame me?
Will you assign me the part of the wayward woman
and never give me a second glance?

Can you say you have never been tempted
by youthful flesh
by the savour of goodness
by the lure of power?

Say you have never tried your own power
to tarnish the glory of another

Whoever is without sin
let them cast the first stone
I'll catch it and throw it back

The prostitute's story

Luke 15.11–32

The first time, I was caught by his young and beautiful body,
by the shyness in his manner
as he lay in my arms afterwards, resting.

The second time, I noticed his accent.
A stranger travelling far from home.

The third time he came to me with hunger in his eyes
and a quiet desperation in the silent thrustings of his body.

The fourth time he cried like a baby missing its mother,
and I rocked him wordlessly.
He didn't want the sex so much as the nearness of my flesh.

The fifth time he started talking and didn't stop till he'd told me
    the whole sad tale.
I told him, 'Swallow your pride, go on home, back where you
    belong.
They'll be glad to see you, believe me.'

So I sent him from me back to his own gods,
the arms of his father, his brother's chastisement and his farm.

I was sadder than I knew to see him go.
Not for his body, though, God knows, I'd come to love its
    contours and its sighs.
It was for his friendship and trust I missed him,
and it's the memory of these that still lingers,
long after the shape of his face has begun to fade.

The woman with the flow of blood

Luke 8.42–8

Twelve long years of my life written in blood:
not the regular, cyclical bleedings other women know, marking out
    the months.
My bleeding was insistent, incessant, in season and out of season,
my womb emptying itself in a ceaseless rending
until it seemed there was nothing left to spill.

It wasn't so much the pain that plagued me, or even the shame.
It was the sheer unmitigated exhaustion,
my soul anaemic as a white bone,
not one tiny tributary of energy or spark of creativity
running anywhere within me.

How I dragged myself up that morning and out to follow the
    crowds I'll never know.
It was as if I was sleep-walking or watching someone else shuffling
    along with the crowd.
I don't even remember lifting my hand to touch him.
But I must have, for he stopped in the same instant and turned to
    face me,
the look of him sending fear and desire coursing in equal measure
    up through my belly,
charging all my body with an intensity I hadn't felt for years.

I was aflame with desire.
Not for *him* but for that magnificent energy coming off his body
    like electricity,
stirring the air until it leaped and crackled blue flame all around
    us
where we stood, two alone amongst hundreds.

His voice commanded me to stand out in the open.
His eyes told me I could make a choice:
for healing, for wholeness, for fullness of life,
for that fire-crackling energy.
If I wanted it badly enough, he seemed to be saying,
it could be mine.

Widow of the disappeared

Luke 18.1–8

What happened to my children?
They are all dead or as good as.
One died from dysentery,
another from the soldier's gun,
a third was maimed by the mines they left in the ground
and can only limp about, one-legged –
he needs my help as much as I need his.
My daughter has moved far away to her husband's village.
They send me what they can manage but it is too far for them to
    visit often.
My husband is long disappeared, whether dead or alive I do not
    know,
taken one night by the military,
and all my kicking and screaming against their guns to no avail.
I am left to scrounge for a living from what scraps I can gather
    from the fields,
or from my neighbours' gardens.
They help me out when they can,
but God knows, they have little enough themselves and too many
    mouths to feed.

I get by.
Every day I walk to the well for water.
Every week I take the slow bus into town
that jiggles my bones about and takes too much of my money.
I make my way to the square where the mothers of the
    disappeared stand,
arms akimbo, placards raised, demanding the return of our
    husbands and children.

It is our need to touch their dear limbs,
to look into their faces,
to smooth their dusty hair,
that drives us here to make our protest.
Every week we dare the taunts of the military,
their guns jabbing our ribs,

their cigarette smoke stinging our eyes.
We know they have taken our names, filed all our details.
They could shoot us at a glance if we step out of line.
But what have we got to lose?
They have taken our husbands and children from us,
there is nothing left in our homes for them to steal.
When there's nothing left for them to take from you,
fear ceases to gnaw away at your bones.

They could kill me, yes, but I'm an old woman near my time
    to die.
I pray I would not falter if they tortured me,
but why would they torture me now?
I have no secrets left to hide.

So every day I walk to the well for water,
every evening I light my candle and pray to the madonna
to uphold all widows and mothers
for she was an abandoned mother herself.
And every week I gather at the square
to protest at the disappearance of our loved ones,
to demand their return.

I refuse to give them the satisfaction of dying.
I refuse the option of a quiet life.
I'm here to stay.

Redemption

But you must never forget the cost:
all that has been lost and will never now be reclaimed;
all the forgotten women whose tales will never now be told;
the pain of generations who never found their own names,
never heard their own voices speaking plain,
women who lived their entire lives long in chains.

And your own gift, in which your heart and body now exults,
    rejoices,
so nearly lost, destroyed, denied, put to death by the fear in you,
those other voices which cried: 'Be like this! Copy us!
Who are you to know what you want, who you are?'
And listening, see how far you travelled in a land that is waste,
tasting nothing but the arid emptiness of your sucked-out soul,
    empty head, muted voice.

This is the loss you sustained, the cost you endured, overcame;
went down far, deep in a foreign land,
stranded way out in motionless time, alien space.
And all the time desperately searching an outstretched hand, a
    familiar face
to lead you out and back up the years and months of wasted time,
    prisoner's fettered pace.

At last she came, spoke your name,
opened her hand, gave you grace,
led you back and up out of that land,
into wild, open time, unbounded space,
a place for you to live and breathe and dance
            again.

Only see, where she stands,
no one else, no one new,
no one known, only you,
only You.

A litany of grief and gladness (1)

For every woman
    whose name is absent from the great traditions of music, art
      and literature,
    whose pictures do not hang in art galleries,
    and whose philosophies and science are not published and read:
      mourning and mercy.
For every woman
    whose artistry is enshrined in anonymous songs, folktales and
      legends,
    whose image is embodied in the face of her children,
    and whose skilled invention is preserved in needlecraft, tapestry
      and patchwork:
      glory and thanksgiving.

For every woman
    refused access to the tools of scholarship,
    excluded from the fraternities of artists
    and forbidden the space of a room of her own:
      mourning and mercy.
For every woman
    who made her own literature in journal, letter and diary,
    who gathered her friends around her for conversation,
    and passed on her wisdom to children and grandchildren:
      glory and thanksgiving.

For every woman
    prevented from exploring her native land,
    precluded from travelling to foreign climes,
    and held back by fear or convention from trekking the wide,
      wide world:
      mourning and mercy.
For every woman
    who made her own home a wide place for welcoming others,
    who encouraged her children to fearless adventure and
      exploration,
    and set no boundaries to her own inner quest for knowledge,
      wisdom and truth:
      glory and thanksgiving.

We grieve for all that has been lost, never to be recovered.
We glory in all that has been recovered, never again to be lost.

A litany of grief and gladness (2)

For every woman
    forbidden to preside at the eucharistic table,
    banned from breaking the holy bread
    and barred from offering the sacred cup:
        mourning and mercy.
For every woman
    who presided at her own supper table,
    who fed the hungry ones with good things
    and succoured the lonely with the cup of life:
        glory and thanksgiving.

For every woman
    denied the right to pronounce absolution,
    forbidden to anoint the sick with holy chrism,
    and prohibited from counselling those in distress:
        mourning and mercy.
For every woman
    who crooned blessing on a sick child,
    whose hands ministered to the dying and brought relief,
    and whose skill administered the healing of touch and
        tenderness:
        glory and thanksgiving.

For every woman
    denied the voice to speak out her own religious truth,
    refused the opportunity to teach her wisdom
    and ridiculed for her theological insights and ideas:
        mourning and mercy.
For every woman
    who claimed her authority in vision, prophecy and dream,
    who spoke out her truth in hymnody, verse and story,
    and cherished the privilege of prayer and knowledge of the
        divine:
        glory and thanksgiving.

We grieve for all that has been lost, never to be recovered.
We glory in all that has been recovered, never again to be lost.

Reclaiming the names

They called us Hag, Crone, Witch and Shrew,
because they feared our knowledge and would not receive our
wisdom.
They called us Spinster, Man-Hater, Old Maid,
because they feared our separateness and envied our self-
chosenness.

*We are reclaiming the names with honour and fierceness,
without shame.*

They called us Magdalene, Temptress, Whore,
because they lusted after our fleshliness and could not resist their
own concupiscence.
They called us Vixen, Cow, Bird and Bitch,
because they feared our sexuality and wished to deny the
sacredness of physicality.

*We are reclaiming the names with honour and fierceness,
without shame.*

They called us Gorgon, Medusa, Hysteric,
because they feared our ferociousness and envied our imaginative
extravagance.
They called us Virago, Battle-axe, Fury,
because they found our strength formidable and our spirits
indomitable.

*We are reclaiming the names with honour and fierceness,
without shame.*

They called us Gossip, Tittle-Tattler, Prattler,
because they feared the power of our telling and envied the ease of
our conversation.
They called us Scribbler, Poetess, Lady Writer,
because they feared our creativity and felt threatened by our
fecundity.

We are reclaiming the names with honour and fierceness, without shame.

They called us the Second Sex, Stranger, Woman,
because they would not embrace our difference,
could not yield to our otherness and feared to receive our giftedness.

We reclaim the names, use their abuse for good,
recast the dye, reweave the words.
Whatever they have called us we receive and renege and renew.
We rework their ancient power to hurt and chide, to hide and revile us.
Their names cannot annihilate us though they have sought to crucify us.
We shall remember them and revive them
in the fire of our passion and our lives.

Chapter 7

This Woman's Body

The body, flesh, senses

A number of years ago I had a hysterectomy. The experience of major surgery, in and of itself, is a very common one, but no less profound for that. It is a liminal experience of giving over one's body and being entirely into the hands of others, going down into the mini-death of anaesthesia, submitting to the surgeon's knife, and coming up the other side into new life as helpless as a kitten; having to learn, like a newborn baby, the bodily basics – how to move, how to urinate and defecate, how to take food, put one foot in front of the other. I cannot be alone in having found this an immensely powerful experience of death and resurrection, of stripping and of revivifying, and of needing to make some kind of spiritual, as well as emotional and psychological, sense out of it all. Yet in 45 years of church attendance, I have never once heard a sermon on the experience of surgery or hospitalization.

Over and beyond the experience of surgery was the very specific challenge of facing the loss of my womb. This confronted me with a complex set of feelings and reactions: the finality of never being able to have children; the end of my years of menstrual bleeding; an inchoate sense of some significant change taking place in my gendered and sexual identity. I needed to mourn these losses and reflect on the changes my body and self were undergoing. I registered the painful irony pointed out by some feminist theologians: that, whereas the liturgy of the Church focuses massive symbolic attention on the body and blood of Christ in the eucharist and on the cross, the bodies and blood of ordinary men and most particularly women have not been seen as holy, sacred or worthy of loving reverence and attention. Indeed, women's bodies and blood have been regarded as taboo, unclean, a source of defilement or, at the very least, distraction from the things of God. This is a travesty of the gospel, a blasphemy against the God who took flesh in Christ and thereby honoured and sacralized all human bodies.

A major theme in feminist liturgy and spirituality has therefore been the reclaiming of women's bodies, the articulation of the taboo subjects of women's sexuality, bleeding, birth-giving, ageing and bodily changes. In an obvious sense, all of the pieces in this collection are written out of the experience of 'this woman's body', but the extracts in this chapter focus in a specific way on the body as a subject of spiritual and theological significance, and as a site of pleasure and pain, wounding and blessing. There is an implicit affirmation here that God is to be known, worshipped and adored, not in spite of the body and sensual knowing but precisely in and through them.

This woman's body

In preparation for a hysterectomy

This woman's body of mine
has never been named or known or held as sacred
in the ritual language or thinking of my church.
Yet she contains knowledge that is deep
                     and secret
                     and powerful
                     and mysterious
and I would speak her now:

This is my body, this is my blood.

This woman's body of mine
which has always been growing and changing and shedding and
    ripening
is forever gifting me with her wisdom
speaking to me and telling me
  how to live my life
  how to know my truth
  how to claim my worth
and I would speak these things now:

This is my body, this is my blood.

This woman's body of mine
holds so many unspoken secrets
  in her hidden, dark places
  her unexplored cavities and crevices
  her inner organs and workings
  her sources of pain and of pleasure
  her bleedings, fluids and secretions, odours and fragrancies
  her unnoticed swellings, tightenings, loosenings and releasings,
  her ungloried galaxy of genes, cells and hormones
    constantly gathering and dispersing
    in the evershifting play of rhythms and cycles.
And I would name this knowledge now:

This is my body, this is my blood.

This woman's body of mine
never ceases to amaze me
with her capacity for feeling, instinctual knowing, intuition and
    sensibility:
  the ecstasy of orgasm and the agony of pain
  the delicacy of touch and the deprivation of hunger
  the fragility of hurting and the potency of anger
  the satisfaction of fullness and the yearning of emptiness
  the tautness of tension and the slackness of sleep
  the pull and push of activity and resting
  the ebb and flow of moon and tide
  the swell and shedding of the belly's capabilities
  the faithfulness and fertility of her patterning and fashioning.
For these and all her myriad moods
and the seasons of her waxing and waning
I would bless her now:

This is my body, this is my blood.

There is so much this woman's body of mine
has never known:
  the abuse of violation
  the degradation of poverty
  the despoliation of conquest or invasion
  the mutilation of war and pillage and rape
  and the weight of a baby in her belly
  the spilling of a body from between her legs
  the pull of a mouth on milk-filled breasts
  the tug of a life on her overflowing heart
  the long, tangled years of mothering, cherishing, separating,
    never separating
  and the comfort of growing old with a mate
And for all these curses and blessings which she has never known,
I hold and honour her now:

This is my body, this is my blood.

This woman's body of mine
which has changed and is changing and will never cease her
    changing

is about to be changed in a radical, unpredictable way.
   The heart of her will be cut open
   the centre of her will be invaded
   the life-giving cup of her will be consumed
   the belly broken into, the treasure mined and seized.

And I am fearful and I am trusting
I am grieving and I am accepting
I am blazing and I am quiet
I am seeing and I am all unknowing
I am crying for the loss of my beautiful baby
I am grieving for the stripping of my flesh
I am wounded with the passing of my time for birthing
I am hurting with the haemorrhaging of my womb
And I am trusting my body's wisdom
I am listening to her calling
I am heeding the many voices of her crying
I am celebrating the many faces of her passing and unpassing
   beauty

So I will speak again my body's bounty
I will name my body's knowledge
I will praise my body's courage
I will eat of her flesh
I will drink of her blood
I will receive at her hands
   of the life-giving death and the death-dealing life
And I will know her as sacred
                         and honoured
                         and highly favoured
                         and chosen
                         and God-taken, blessed, broken and
                              offered,
for

This is my body, this is my blood.

Prayer of a childless woman

Though this belly has never swollen with the burden of a baby,
let me grow big with the longing for justice which shall be for all
the children of God.

Though these breasts have never suckled an infant,
let my largesse of love nurture those who are hungry for the feast
of life.

Though these arms have never cradled my own child,
let them reach out tenderly to those who pine for a mother's love.

Though these lips have never spoken my own baby's name,
let me croon blessing and balm and healing on many a charmless,
unlullabied life.

Though this mind has never imagined my own child's life,
may I dream dreams for children whose prospects are pitiful and
whose hopes are slender.

And though I have wept over my unborn child's unfulfilled
possibilities,
may I never be so absorbed in my own small griefs that I have not
the compassion
to weep with the motherless child and to mourn with the childless
mother
to grieve with the abandoned infant and to rage over the stillborn
babe
to sorrow over the squandered life and to lament over each
uncherished son and daughter.

And may I offer these arms
and may I open this heart
and may I proffer this body
to each baby screaming for justice
each child reaching for love
each neighbour longing for mercy
each mother mourning the useless spilling of blood.

For childless and child-bearing we belong together
Solitary and companioned we are of the one blood
Mothers and spinsters we are of the same lineage
We are each offspring of the body of God.

Red

Every month, the spurt and stain of blood:
a veritable flood
streaming down my legs,
uncheckable by towel or swaddling cloth,
like the gush of life wreaked by a murdering sword
in the hands of a wrathful god.
Thick, glutinous clots of red
like rope in my hand
are all that is left of the life that is gone.
Yet this bleeding body and gaping womb
bear other kinds of fruit.
The thick issue of blood
releases a torrent of words,
a juice of speech,
a tidal wave of poems:
food for the children of other women's
bellies, milk for the babes
suckled by other women's breasts.

So celebrate the red of spilt
passion, poetry, prodigality:
uncheckable tide of blood
that is good,
that is food,
that is fecund river of life.
Each month,
the flushing out of flesh,
the death that issues in life,
the feast of blood,
the flood that is God.

Wilgefortis and her sisters

To begin you learn to hate your chin:
the line of the jaw, the firmness of its set,
the growing slackness over the years.
This will take many moons but starts early in most of the race.

You must listen to the voice of that first boyfriend
who chides you gently for the delicate layer of down
that teases the line of your jaw.
You see the mocking in his eyes, you read his meaning.

Without even knowing you are doing it,
over many years you must watch hoarding boards, reel in
   TV adverts,
soak yourself in magazine glossies
of thin, beautiful women with sleek heads of hair
and never a single sprouting follicle
under the arms, on the legs,
oh never on the face.
This is the norm, the form you must aspire to,
tirelessly pressing yourself into its mould.

You must learn to become stranger
to your own body's odours, contours, shadings.
You must panic at the slightest gesture of growth
where it should not, must not be.
You must cut it back ruthlessly,
razor it, shave it, pluck it, scour and cream it away.
You must apply the make-up thickly
to cover the place where you removed the hairs,
the face you've grown ashamed to bear.

If you continue like this over months and years,
endlessly shaving it back,
it will grow more thickly,
it will sprout in new places,
the hairs will come coarser and darker.
At last, when you abandon the battle
with the animal inside of you

who won't be groomed, tamed,
fashioned into domesticity,
and put the razor down

you'll become the abominable woman
the two-headed monster
the freak of nature
the walking abhorrence to all men
the inestimably mysterious
lady with the beard.

Writing the body

Write the body:
every curve, every nerve, every cell
deserves to be heard,
to be spelled into word, into being.
Mouth her flesh into firm, choice words,
full and round-bellied.
Let the body speak.

Right the body:
untwist, uncurl, unfold
from the tortured conundrums
forced and foisted
for years on her frame.
Throw off the frozen form
she's been locked into
these too long, too cold years.
Unfold. Unbend.
Let her breathe.
Let her mend her ancient ways.
Let her befriend herself again.
Let her live her own
deep, dark and dangerous truth.
She cannot lie.

Rite the body:
sing, dance, fling the body into sacred space.
Charm her, chant her,
cast her into woman-time and pace.
Spell her name.
In this grace she will be born again, over and over.
No stopping her now.
She is bounding out of sight, out of bounds,
like some roaring lioness prowling
the sheer immensity of all space, all time,
leaping the galaxies between the stars.
For there is no stopping her now:
she is coming to herself,
coming into herself,
she is coming
over and over again.

Graces

A summer fruits grace

I will eat this cherry as if it were the first and last from the tree.
I will savour this peach as if it were the only one.
I will relish this mango as if it were the harvest of paradise.
I will worship this fruit as if it were the body of God.

A grace after sickness

After vomiting, I rise and eat again.
The food that I could not stomach yesterday
tastes of earth and heaven.
I chew bread slowly.
I sip water.
I marvel that I am upright.
It is enough.

A grace for eating alone

Blessed be the silence of this meal.
Blessed be the solitude of this eating.
Blessed be the company of unseen presences.
Blessed be my single table.

God bless the backs

God bless the backs that ache from working in the fields.
God bless the hands that smart from labouring in the factories.
God bless the fingers that burn from cooking over the fire.
God bless our bodies that will consume the sacrifice of others'
  lives.

Blessing of the senses

For Isabel and Elise

May your eyes be bright
and, though they should fail you in old age and your vision
    become dimmed,
may your inner sight grow sharper and your vision of God's
    kingdom clearer
  with the passing of the years.

May your ears be open
and, though they should fail you in old age and become blocked,
may your listening grow more attentive and your attunement to
    God's voice more discerning
  with the passing of the years.

May your nose be unerring
and, though it should fail you in old age and become dulled,
may the memory of the sweet smells of God's earth never be
    diminished
and the aroma of God's loveliness deepen in you
  with the passing of the years.

May your mouth be firm
and, though it should fail you in old age and your appetite become
    jaded,
may your hunger for justice grow more intensely and your taste
    for goodness sweeten daily
  with the passing of the years.

May your hands and feet be steady
and, though they should fail you in old age and become gnarled,
may your touch always be gentle
and your hold always be loving
and your living always be tender
and your journey towards God's beauty remain unfaltering
  with the passing of the years.

And now may God fill all your senses with the joy of divine
    gladness
and the yearning which surpasses every longing
until your eyes at last shall see the beauty
and your ears shall hear the music
and your nose shall inhale the aroma
and your mouth shall taste the sweetness
and your arms and body shall feel the tenderness of the embrace
    of the Beloved
and every sense in you shall be satisfied and silenced
  in the passing of these years and the consummation of your
    lives.

Chapter 8

So Many Kinds of Awesome Love

Solidarity, connection, loving

Christian tradition has honoured and valorized certain forms of human relationship: heterosexual marriage, the bond of parent and child within the family, the duty of filial care, the service of God in the needy other, the communal living out of the vowed celibate life. At the same time, other forms of human loving and connection have been ignored, accorded lesser value or stigmatized altogether: the bonds of friendship, particularly those between women; the pursuit of justice as a form of right relation; the solidarity that can extend across differences of many kinds – ethnic, cultural, religious and so on; and, of course, the erotic, sexual love that may flourish between persons of the same sex.

In this chapter, I seek to name and celebrate some of the 'many kinds of awesome love' that have been important to me, and through which I have known incarnated something of the many-splendoured, awesome love of God. If it seems peculiar that I have included 'A psalm of solitude' in this section, it is because I have spent a good deal of my adult life as a single, celibate woman living alone, and it is within this solitary condition that I have learnt a great deal of what it means both to give and receive love, and to love God both above and within all other loves. I have also fallen deeply in love and known what it is to be loved in return: desired and cherished by the human lover who, at the best, may also be partner, helper, co-worker, sister, brother, friend. A number of the poems in this section are celebrations of erotic, sexual love in which the intimacy and mystery of divine love is touched in a particularly intense, bodily way. Then there is the love of friends, both near and far, both old and new, which is perhaps the love that has been the most constant and enduring in my life, alongside that of family, outlasting broken romances, the changes and chances of working relationships, the shifting constellations of solitariness and con-nectedness. Friends are those whose faithfulness teaches me deeply about the enduring, steadfast love of God.

Whatever the forms and faces of loving, there is a growing sense in my life of the profound interconnectedness at the heart of reality: that all, whoever and whatever our condition, however strange or different we may perceive each other to be, are made for one another in love and friendship:

> For childless and child-bearing we belong together
> Solitary and companioned we are of the one blood
> Mothers and spinsters we are of the same lineage
> We are each offspring of the body of God.

So many kinds of awesome love

1 Corinthians 13

There are so many kinds of awesome love,
I bless them all:

Love of kindred for their kin
Love of lover for their mate
Love of country for the native
Love of land for the explorer

Love of the labourer for his work
Love of the scholar for her truth
Love of the artist for the muse
Love of the preacher for the word
Love of the disciple for the way
Love of the mystic for their God

There are so many kinds of awesome love,
We need them all:

Love of brother, sister, father, mother
Love of parent, grandparent, uncle, aunt
Love of the beloved, love of the friend,
Love of the stranger, love of the needy

Love of the woman for the man
Love of the man for the woman
Love of woman for her woman
Love of the man for his man

There are so many kinds of awesome love,
Why must we set one above the other,
Say some are worthy and others base?
Why must we choose one love
When we need all the kinds we can get?

There are so many kinds of awesome love:
The love that knocks you off your feet
  and sets you to desperate things
The love that is gentle and kind
  and swells the compassionate heart
The love that is joyous and life-giving
  and keeps you singing for days
The love that is steadfast and loyal
  and sits out long nights of pain

Young, jocular love
Old, wise love
Rich, extravagant love
Poor, pitiful love
Strong, encouraging love
Vulnerable, wounded love
Passionate, sensual love
Free, filial love
Fiery, prophetic love
Self-emptied, contemplative love

There are so many kinds of awesome love,
I bless them all.

Weaving of the cloth: an Advent canticle

We are making a cloth for Christ's cradle;
we are weaving a covering for the child to be born.

We are working into this cloth
  the words of our conversations,
  the silences of our sleeping,
  the wordlessness of our praying,
  the music of our singing.

We are bringing the strands of our many rivalries, jealousies and
    hurtings.
We are offering the tautness of our anxiety, exhaustion and
    overburdenedness.
We are relinquishing the threads of our pettinesses, obsessions and
    prejudices.
We are confessing the tangles of our confusions, inadequacies and
    misunderstandings.

We are making a cloth for Christ's cradle;
we are weaving a covering for the child to be born.

We are bringing exotic silks and rich brocades.
We are bringing simple cottons and rough hessian.
We are offering the rich man's garb and the poor child's tatters.
We are offering the privileged woman's robes and the destitute
    baby's rags.

We are weaving the strong threads and the fragile threads.
We are braiding the dark strands and the bright strands.
We are knitting together the tough and the tender.
We are working the painful and the joyful.

We are making a cloth for Christ's cradle;
we are weaving a covering for the child to be born.

We are working these strands into the one cloth:
  a cloth fit for a newborn,
  a covering fashioned for the child of our flesh,
  an offering to God who is our kith and our kin.

We are making a cloth for Christ's cradle;
we are weaving a covering for the child to be born.

Blessing at the table

As the many threads are made one in the cloth,
as the many grains are made one in the bread,
as the many grapes are made one in the wine,
so we who are many are made one
as we stand around this table
laid with the one cloth
and set with the one cup
and fed with the one loaf.

Psalm of solitude

May my solitude be fruitful,
like a tree which is planted by streams of water,
whose branches yield their fruit in due season,
and whose leaves do not wither.
May my solitude be fruitful.

May my solitude be stable,
like a rock set high above the waters,
which stands and does not crumble,
and is a place of refuge amidst the floods and tempests.
May my solitude be stable.

May my solitude be truthful,
like a book which lies open
in which all may read the pages of your wisdom
and the secrets of your mercy
and the searching of your ways.
May my solitude be truthful.

May my solitude be prayerful,
like a well whose depths cannot be fathomed
which offers its clear and thirst-quenching waters
to those who will search in her darkness.
May my solitude be prayerful.

May my solitude be spacious
like a broad place into which you lead me,
where my spirit exults and my body rejoices,
where I may dance alone and in the company of others.
May my solitude be spacious.

May my solitude be joyful
and sing out its singular witness,
like birdsong at dawn and day's ending,
which is pure, spontaneous and lovely,
filled with the gratitude of all creation
for the simplicity of living and the glory of being alive.
May my solitude be joyful.

Thanksgiving for friends

These, these are the ones who have walked with me
where no others would come.
These are the ones who have not refused to look upon me.
These are the ones who have come near.

These are the ones who have shown me your face.
These are the ones who have touched me with your nearness.
These are the ones who have incarnated your justice.
These are the ones who have mediated your presence.

I am trembling.
I am thankful.

You

When they walked away from me, one by one,
You, you still stood standing.

When they would not look at me,
Your eyes held me steadily and did not turn away.

When they could not tell me what they had done,
would not speak it face to face,
you named their action without dissembling, without caricature,
without falsehood.

When they would not touch me or welcome my kind,
You, you enfolded me in arms as wide as a mother's.

When my flesh was abhorrent to them so that they would not
   come near,
You stayed with me
   you sat with me
   you lay with me.

When fear was in the air and the cowardice of an easy truce,
your courage emblazoned me
your outrage steadied me
your truthfulness anchored me.

Now they are gone and, though I am alone,
You are still with me,
my friends,
my lover,
my truthful ones.

I do not know how I shall go on,
but you will teach me, you will watch over me.
And God in you.

Charis

You touched my flesh
with infinitely tender embrace:
the touch of charis,
the caress of grace,
the chrism of bliss.

You sought my face with your lips,
came closer than breathing
to give me the kiss of peace.
No one loved me like this.

You opened my body
like rain parting leaves,
like the blessing of oil
on a dying man's brow.
You blessed, broke and offered
the bread of your body.
You ate of my flesh,
you drank of my juice.
You forsook every other
and cleaved unto me.
We are flesh of one flesh.
We are forged of one will.
We are still,
in the heart,
in the bone,
in the dark,
in the tongueless,
wondering place
where two are made one.
We are gift,
we are grace,
we are the face of love.
We are one, we are one.

Making love with you

Is being born again
Is dying and rising to a new world
Is heaven come on earth

Is softness
and sweetness
and soaring
and the silence of holy prayer

Is wetness
and warmth
and wonder

Is tenderness
is trembling
is a torrent

You are the ground on which I stand
You are the air I breathe
You are the sky towards which I climb

You are my holy sacrament
          my sacred food
          my only good
We are the eucharistic feast
This is the divine mystery
of God made manifest in flesh
She is with us
in the body
in the blood
We are holy good
We are fecund god

With you

With you
I am cherished
I am lavished
I am ravished

With you
I am at ease
I am at peace
I am released

With you
I am utterly natural
I am entirely comfortable
I am undoubtedly adorable

With you
I am discovered
I am uncovered
I am recovered

With you
I feel no need to hide
I am open wide
I am fully alive

With you
I am a goddess
I am so glamorous
I am quite fabulous

With you
I am wholly me
I am everything I've ever been
I am all I shall yet be

Banquet

Song of Songs 2.4

Like water in the desert you quenched my thirst
Like wine in winter you warmed my belly
Like milk from the breast you satisfied my hunger
Like manna in the wilderness you filled my longing

You were sweet new bread from the oven to my mouth
You were ripe sun-drenched peach to my lips
You were golden lather of honey thick on my tongue
You were clean running water cool on my fingers

All my heart's longing is made known to you
My body's quickening thirst cannot be hidden from you
You sensed the fainting of my flesh and caught me fast in your
   arms
You lifted my drooping frame and set me at your table of delights

You feasted me right royally at your banquet overflowing with
   riches
You fêted me fondly at your table with your dazzling presence
Until I was full to overflowing
Sated with the sweetness of your love

I am consumed with the taste of your kisses
Drunk with the perfume of your skin
You have fed me with the riches of heaven
You have filled me with the banquet of God

Collects

Luke 15.11–32

God of unconditional love,
long before we were ready you ran to meet us
and embraced us;
when we did not deserve it
you lavished your love upon us.
Teach us how to receive your embrace
and extend it, with compassion and generosity,
to the others we find it hard to forgive.

Luke 18.1–8

God of the defenceless little ones
whose name and nature is love:
Enable us to use what power we have
to speak and act for the rights of those denied justice
and, when the cause of right seems to go unheeded,
give us the persistence to keep on pestering
until righteousness prevails.

Song of Songs

God of all love and longing,
whose beauty is traced
in the body of each beloved:
Reach out to us in every impulse towards connection
that we may discern your loveliness
in every movement of human loving.

Chapter 9

All Golden Peach

Joy, celebration, praise

The joy of sense, the joy of colour and sight, the joy of taste, the joy of loving and being loved, the joy when life flows in and through one as a song or a dance, without effort, without struggle, without labour – these are some of the joys celebrated by the pieces in this chapter. There is, too, a certain joy in struggle, the joy that is part of working for something one passionately believes in, the joy of being able to muster all one's energies and abilities in the service and affirmation of something bigger than one's own tiny ego, something or someone worthy of effort, of costly adoration, worship and praise. Whatever the source or reason for joy, to feel joy is to be fully alive in every fibre of one's being, to be aware of body and soul working together in harmony, to have the sense of being utterly at home in one's self, in one's body, in one's place in the world, if only for a brief moment. Such a capacity for joy is, I believe, intimately related to the capacity and willingness to experience to the full the realities of anger, sadness, anguish and longing for wholeness of which I have already written in earlier chapters. Both the capacity for joy and the capacity for pain are twin sides of the one reality which has to do with a certain openness, a certain transparency, to life in all its fullness (a fullness containing both ecstasy and agony) and to the other (both human and divine) who may wound and bless in equal measure.

While joy is an emotion received at particular moments in life, largely beyond one's choice or control, praise is something different. Praise is a willed, intentional activity to bless, to honour and to sacralize in the blessing, some person or activity and, above all, God who is the source of all blessing and goodness. As such, praise may be offered at any moment and in any mood, out of anguish and suffering as well as in joy and peace. We worship, we praise and adore in the last analysis simply because God is who and what God is and we are creatures made for adoration.

Some of the pieces in this chapter were written for particular personal celebrations – a fortieth birthday, a name-day for a religious – while others were occasioned by more ordinary, recurrent pleasures – the pleasures of eating food or walking by the sea. Others were written for communal celebration; in particular, the gathering of the Christian community for the great thanksgiving and adoration of the eucharist, that central act of worship which orients and renews Christians in their gratitude for the continual offering of God's self to God's world in creation, redemption and sustenance. Yet, in a wider sense I would want to say that every act of thanksgiving or praise is intrinsically eucharistic insofar as it realizes the very blessing it invokes. Whenever we take words of praise and blessing upon our lips and utter them aloud, we not only express our existing joy and pleasure, we also make more joy and pleasure to abound in the world, both for our own, for others' and for God's greater delight.

Word

St Mary's Abbey, West Malling

Wait for the riven word.
It will be spoken, it will be heard.
It is the time for speech,
the bursting wide of flesh.
Like golden juice from the ripened peach,
it will spill, it will pour,
it will run down your famished face.

Feast your lips on this food.
Fill your mouth with this fruit.
Feed your soul on this fat.
It is good. It is god.
It is food of life,
the fountain of speech,
the word that satisfies.

O come and eat, o taste and see:
How good a feast.
How rich a guest.
How lavish a host.
How ravished a hunger.
I am met. I am meat. I am ate.
I am full. I am fed.
I am juice, I am joy, I am all golden peach.
I am flesh of your flesh,
bone of my own solid bone.
I am word. I am spoken.
I am food. I am eaten.
I am incarnate, holy bread.
I am born.
     I am come.
         I am home.

A canticle of celebration

For a fortieth birthday celebration

Celebrate life in the midst
     in the middle
     in the muddle

Celebrate life in the storm
     in the strife
     in the struggle

Celebrate life in the chaos
     in the confusion
     in the catastrophes

Celebrate life in the joy
     in the gentleness
     and generosity

Celebrate life in its pain
     in its paralysis
     in its poverty

Celebrate life in its energy
     in its exuberance
     in its ecstasy

Celebrate life in its darkness
     in its dyings
     in its departures

Celebrate life in its labour
     in its laughter
     in its loveliness

Celebrate life in all its magnificence,
     multiplicity and mystery:
     unbiddable
     unstoppable
     unquenchable.

A canticle in praise of work

Celebrate the labour of toil
  all scrubbing and scouring
  all sweeping and dusting
  all cooking and serving
  all feeding and feasting
  all planting and pruning
  all mending and making
  all hammering and heaving
  all building and constructing

Celebrate the labour of love
  all listening and discerning
  all comforting and cradling
  all holding and embracing
  all nurturing and nourishing
  all cherishing and chiding
  all watching and waiting
  all hearing and healing
  all encouraging and enabling

Celebrate the labour of creation
  all daring and dreaming
  all imagining and inventing
  all kindling and inspiring
  all gestating and germinating
  all labouring and birthing
  all shaping and forming
  all risking and ruminating
  all releasing and relinquishing

Celebrate the labour of justice
  all sharing and resourcing
  all protesting and proclaiming
  all struggling and standing
  all campaigning and challenging
  all marching and militancy
  all organizing and orchestrating
  all refusing and resisting
  all holding on and hoping

Graces

1

For the grace of living
For the grace of savouring
For the grace of God
       in our lives
       at our table
       in our bodies
Thanks be

2

How did I come to be seated at this table?
How did I come to be eating of this bread?
I am not worthy that you should serve me
yet I will sit and eat.

3

I handle this bowl with respect
I lift this cup with reverence
I wipe this plate with thankfulness
I receive this food with gratitude

   From you, mother earth
   From you, brother human
   From you, father time
   From you, sister sustenance

I worship

4

For the candle that gives its light
For the rose that proffers its perfume
For the hands that offer their labour
For the friends who share their fellowship
For the food that makes our sustenance
Thanks be to God.

5

Whoever plucked these fruits, may they be blessed.
Whoever sorted and cleaned, packaged and prepared these foods,
        may they be blessed.
Whoever dreamed the recipes, concocted the flavours,
    experimented with the mixtures,
        may they be blessed.
Whoever chopped or mashed, sautéed or pureed; whipped, beat or
    folded; fried, baked or poached,
        may they be blessed.
And whoever eats, with appetite large or small, body young or old,
        may we, too, be blessed.

Abbey praise

For Mary John on her name day

For the empty cup and the cup brimming over,
for the famished soul and the soul that is feasted,
for the sleeping heart and the heart that is wakened,
  blessed be God!

From the chattering mind and the gathered thoughts,
from the tossing limbs and the steady breath,
from the restless heart and the heart brought to rest,
  blessed be God!

With the stammering lips and the stilled tongue,
with the writing hand and the hand that lies waiting,
with the beating heart and the heart that has ceased its beating,
  blessed be God!

In the speeding time and the time slowed to one moment,
in the turning wheel and the stillness at the centre of the turning,
in the dancing feet and the timeless rest at the heart of the dancing,
  blessed be God!

Broken night and mended day, blessed may you be!
Bitter cold and golden sun, blessed may you be!
Time out of joint and time in tune, blessed may you be!

All grief and gain,
all joy and pain,
all seasons of mourning,
all times of returning,
all steps of the dance,
all turnings of chance,
all lament and loss,
all sides of the cross,
  blessed may you be
  and blessed be God's name for ever!

Eucharistic prayer

(Sections in square brackets are optional.)

God is with us:
Alleluia!

Lift up heads, hearts, hands:
To the God of all glory we raise them!

Glory to you, Creator God,
you mother all things into being:
earth-stone and moon-dust,
molten lava and fissured rock,
ocean depths and mountain heights.
Amongst the splendour of your creation,
you fashion creatures to show forth your beauty,
and a people to live out your truth.
You welcome and nourish each one into life:
dolphin and dog-rose,
swallow and sword-fish,
human and hippopotamus.
In each you display your particularity:
the simple and the complex,
the hidden and the manifest,
the infinitesimal and the immense,
the tender new-born and the wrinkled well-worn ones.
None to you is alien or unchosen,
all are children of your love.
Glory to you, Creator God!

Glory to you, Incarnate God,
you come and tabernacle among us,
sharing our flesh and our ways.
Living among us,
you taste our hunger,
you share our sufferings,
you inhabit our longings.
Learning to know us,
you touch our faces,

you speak our names,
you eat and drink at our tables.
Longing to empower us,
you reveal God among us,
nearer than breathing,
closer than touching,
yet stranger than knowing,
fiercer than loving.
Glory to you, Incarnate God!

Glory to you, Sustainer God,
you kindle, protect and encourage life in all things,
you are the presence and the dynamic of love in the world.
As holy fire, you inflame the world
with the longing for freedom and justice,
never letting us rest in plenty or despair in poverty.
As sacred truth, you inspire prophets, sages and saints of all times
    and places
to discern and interpret your mysterious ways.
As mighty wind, you empower the Church to live out the life of
    the gospel,
blowing within and beyond the boundaries we set for your
    working.
As enduring presence, you keep alive in the hearts of the faithful
the memory of God's saving actions
and the hope of the fulfilment of God's purposes.
Glory to you, Sustainer God!

[Called into being by God our Creator,
called into loving by God our Redeemer,
called into labour by God our Sustainer,
we gather together now around this table:]

[We are needy for your grace and your mercy:
Take the towel, Christ, and serve us!
We are ready for your healing and your cleansing:
Bring the bowl, Christa, and wash us!
We are longing for your presence and your touch:
Set the table, Christ, and sit with us!

We are waiting for the renewal of our lives:
Call the chosen, Christa, and sup with us!
We are hungry for your truth and your word:
Break the bread, Christ, and feed us!
We are thirsty for your life and your love:
Pour the wine, Christa, and satisfy us!]

As we gather together at the table,
we remember our blessed brother Jesus,
who feasted and fêted among us,
who shared the scraps of our poverty
and the bread of our plenty.
On the night on which he was betrayed,
he gathered his friends together
to share the last meal before his death.
He took bread, gave blessing, broke the loaf and said:
'This is my body, which is for you.
Do this to remember me.'
And the cup, too, he offered to them, saying:
'This cup is the new covenant in my blood.
Do this, whenever you drink it,
to remember me.'

Come now, God our Creator, Redeemer and Sustainer:
send your Spirit to bend over this bread and this wine,
and over us as we gather round them.
Warm us with your life-giving breath.
Suckle us with your nourishing breast.
Enlarge us with your passionate love for the world.
Feed us now with your bread
so that, nourished ourselves,
we may go forth to nourish others.
Quench our thirst here with your wine
so that, satisfied ourselves,
we may share our table with others.
Impassion our hearts now with your fire,
so that, enflamed ourselves,
we may set your creation ablaze
with the fire of your truth and justice.

The breaking of the bread

Breaking this bread, we offer our own brokenness
to be united with the broken body of Christ and of Christ's world.

Pouring out this wine, we pour out our own generosity
to be united with the shed blood of Christ and the Spirit's
outpouring.

The sharing of the bread and cup

Bread for a hungry people, wine for a thirsty world.
Come eat, come drink, at the banquet of the Beloved.

Post-communion prayer

For the gathering at your table,
O God, we praise you.
For the feeding at your table,
O Christ, we bless you.
For the renewing at your table,
O Spirit, we worship you.
May we who have gathered
go now to gather the fragments of a broken world.
May we who have been fed
go now to feed others.
May we who have been renewed
go now to work for the renewal of the whole creation.

In the power and presence of God,
Creator, Redeemer and Sustainer, we go!

Chapter 10

The Edge of God

Re-imaging the divine

In the small writing group to which I belong, we were challenged one week to write around the notion of 'The edge of God'. There is a sense in which *any* writing or speaking of God can only be an edging close and then a veering off again, a fumbling after hints, shadows and guesses, a groping in the dark. Christian tradition has at times seemed far too certain of itself and of its affirmation of the names and nature of God. Yet Christianity has also hallowed the apophatic way, the way of silence, negation and paradox in which we can only stutter 'Not this, not this' and every positive image must be cancelled out by its opposite. One of the gifts of feminist theology is the way in which it subverts and destabilizes the hegemony of patriarchal images of God: God the ruling king, judge, lord and so on. Feminist and other liberation traditions offer a plethora of new, or recovered, images for God and enable us to bring many names to God's worship and service. In this final chapter, I offer some of my own attempts to 'bring many names' to the encounter with divine mystery. God is here imaged as stroppy middle-aged woman, as hiker, as spinster, quester, jester, as the dark but comely lover in the Song of Solomon, as mysterious, unnamed presence in darkness and winter, as the One encountered in every human worker, neighbour, stranger, fool and friend.

In my writing and praying, I find myself returning, again and again, to two particular root metaphors. One is the image of darkness, shadow and unknowing of which I have already written in Chapter 4 (and almost every one of the pieces in that chapter could as well have been placed in this). The other is the image of water – that elusive, dynamic and uncontrollable element into which we are born, both as individuals and as species; that nour-ishes and supports life, that cleanses, that quenches thirst, that carries great ships on its heaving oceans; that, as flood and tempest, can wreak destruction and havoc. This drawing to water is hardly surprising, since I grew up only a mile from the sea and the sounds of its tides and boomings were threaded through my childhood.

No one image or model, however elusive or rich, can do more than offer glimpses and hints towards the divine. The best poems and prayers awaken as much as they satisfy curiosity, desire, the longing for we know not what – the beyond, the Other, the One towards whom we journey and quest in all our human searchings. If any one of the pieces in this collection drives the reader in reignited desire back to the source of all running rivers and life-giving waters, to plunge over the edge of divine darkness, I shall be glad.

The edge of God

What makes God edgy?
Bible bashers,
religious professionals,
intense, pious types
who do their best
to keep her edges
tight, clean,
pristine.

God gets nervous
when she's carless,
can't go out at night
roaming the streets for life,
without risking a ticking off
from the children next morning.

She sits at the breakfast table sulking,
won't tell what she's been up to.
Slips away to her room,
slams the door,
plays her records loud.

Ecclesiastical hedges

Planted in neat, straight lines,
designed to keep divinity in
or the world at bay?
Who can say?
They are thick and intricately tangled,
exquisitely manicured
by God's officials
who have had long training
in the finer arts of hedging.

Snipping this way and that,
they mould the bushy green growth
into ever more ingenious designs:
flying fish, glamorous dragons,
motherly pelicans, tender lions,
meek lambs and impressive eagles.
So engrossed are they
in their tending of theological topiary,
they fail to notice
God popping on her walking gear
and slipping out the back garden gate,
heading for the hills,
quietly whistling.

The kingdom of God

isn't something you could name or quantify or describe

is not a territory or a geography or a landscape
but not *not* any of these either

is fermenting in eggs and money
and guns and roses and glances
in kissing and dancing
and throwing open your household to the strangers
and praying for the Iraqis
and joining the peace marches
and writing the next letter
and cooking the breakfast
and looking for a long time at this painting
and reading a poem
and giggling and smiling and flirting
and planting a juniper tree
and staying for a very long time silent

and becoming angry at this child's lost chances
and weeping over the desert landscape
and trying to be a mother to Jesus
and talking to your own father and brothers and sisters
or trying to, however hard they don't listen

it isn't here or there or anywhere
but it's near and it's far and it comes close just when you think
it's impossibly distant
a chimera on the horizon

the kingdom of God has got to be now
though you know you'll never get there

it isn't something you could write about in a poem
but writing could leave you hungry for it

Welcome the stranger

Matthew 25.31–46

I walk in your streets as	the worker
	the shirker
	the youngster
	the prankster
	the heckler
	the helper
	the stumbler
	the raver
	the foreigner
	the angel
	the fool
	the friend
I come to your door as	the caller
	the neighbour
	the borrower
	the lender
	the maker
	the mender
	the carrier
	the sender
	the Bible-basher
	the well-wisher
	the angel
	the fool
	the friend
I sit at your table as	the nearest
	the dearest
	the uninvited
	the unexpected
	the weary
	the worried
	the hassled
	the hurried
	the talkative

the taciturn
the angel
the fool
the friend

I speak in your heart as the courted
the cursed
the lonely
the loony
the silent
the searching
the discovering
the wounded
the wise one
the angel
the fool
the friend

Where you walk I am walking
where you open I am arriving
where you gather I am meeting
where you listen I am speaking

So welcome stranger and angel
the friend, foe and fool
to your homeland
to your kinfolk
to your lodging
to your table
to your chamber
to your hearth
to your heart

Embrace the stranger in yourself
meet yourself in the stranger
greet your God in the discovery of strangers become friends
and others becoming sisters and brothers

Venetian still life

Round the back of the prison
in a broad, tree-lined avenue
a man lies sleeping, unnoticed, on a bench.
He is stretched out in shadow.
No sunlight touches him.

His trousers are dusty and crumpled,
his trainers stained and scuffed,
yet he is long and lissom in sleep,
his black curly hair soft as a cat's fur,
one olive hand curved under him,
the other falling open to the ground.

Every line and limb of him is elegant,
his silent untouchability more eloquent
than any masterpiece framed in gold
or attended by pouting putti.

No one will paint his face or sculpt his living form.
His image will not appear in the hallways of palaces
or the naves of city churches.
I bow to his presence
as I pass under the shadows of the branches
and return to the tourist thoroughfares.

Spinster God

Spinster God,
weave your strong presence
through the threads of my days:
the warp and the weft,
the dark and the light,
the tangled and the taut,
that the tapestry of my life
may reflect your abundant richness
and stalwart strength.

Quester God

Quester God,
chase your inquisitive presence
through the journey of my days:
its restings and its travellings,
its leavings and its arrivings,
its adventuring and its homecomings,
that the pilgrimage of my life
may unfold your trustworthy faithfulness
and lifegiving companionship.

Jester God

Jester God,
clown your disruptive presence
into the comedy of my days:
its leapings and its tumblings,
its foolishness and its wisdom,
its banality and its solemnity,
that the humour of my life
may reverberate with your healing hilarity
and renewing vivacity.

The water, the fire, the body

After the Benjamin Britten memorial window by John Piper,
in Aldeburgh Parish Church

Source of all verdancy,
make my life green
as the healing river
curving its way to the sea.
And let your curlew cry
be heard over and under its wanderings.

Keeper of the persecuted,
let not the flames of enmity consume my life.
May your angel of mercy
bend over the places of conflagration.
Let the sparks rise in the dark night air,
and let there be fires of justice.

Embracer of those who return,
lay your hands gently on my wounded places.
Let me find a home for this body
whose feet are smarting
whose flesh flinches still
at the expected gesture of rejection.

May every body be healed
in the water
in the fire.

Coming to water

Go to water. It may be lake, river or sea.
It does not matter, so long as the source is clean.
Each makes its own kind of poultice for sickness.
Here you will find healing,
though it may not be in the form you are seeking.

You must build a necessary hunger before you get there.
You must be needy. You must be hurting.
You must be lonely as the seabird's cry
far out near the horizon.

After arriving, you must wait for a long while.
You will still be arriving.

Walk and walk and walk by the water's edge.
Sit for long stretches at a time
gazing out at its many surfaces.
Think of nothing.
Let time and the passages of daylight and darkness
pass over and under you.

If it is dry and the sun beats golden on you,
close your eyes and bask in the miracle of warmth.
If it rains, whether sweetly or fiercely,
let your face be turned upwards to receive its blessing,
your skin be covered in wetness.
If a storm should holler and rage and shake the skies,
walk out in it, let your body be blasted
by an energy that knocks you sideways,
emptying your limbs of all resistance.

You must go to the water.
You must take what it offers.
You must yield what it asks of you.
You must submit to its tenderness.
You must leave when it is time, though it is never time for leaving.
You must walk away still thirsty,
with the sound of its pouring ringing in your ears.

Sea song

You were colour to me:
bladderwrack and wheatsheaf,
blown meadow and metal rust,
mudflat, oyster.

You were time to me:
morning and evening,
seasons swelling, waning, passing,
all time and no time.

You were sound to me:
whimpering, breathing, singing, hollering,
raging. You held the pipit's thin cry,
stone and mountain's fury.
You were the silence under the mountain.

When there were no words you were words to me,
you were ballast and balm when everything was unravelling.
You were god to me in a godless time.
You were gentleness.
You were freezing.

How should I sing of you?
As if to tell of my own blood running, pulse working.
Time past and time passing,
changed, changing, changeless,
ageing and ageless.

All words drown in you,
as flesh and forest do.
Only the fish live in you
and do not know it.

Advent

St Mary's Abbey, West Malling

Under the words you are my silence,
under the river you are my rock,
under the singing you are the voiceless sighing,
under the storm's tumult, you are my ship's safe dock.

Under the winter you are the new season turning,
under the darkness you are the approaching morning,
under the year's ending you are an unseen beginning,
under our Advent you are the Christchild aborning.

Litany to a dark God

Song of Songs 1.5, 6

I hear her voice in the night shadows
but I do not see her face
I feel her breath on the cold night air
but I cannot touch her flesh
Near to me as breathing
intimate as touching
in the darkness she eludes my grasp
she evades my touch
All her ways are strange to me
and all her paths are hidden

She is speaking to me in the darkness
but I do not comprehend what she is saying
She is leading me in the darkness
but I cannot tell where she is moving
She is pursuing me in the darkness
but I cannot discover her purpose

Under the velvet cover of night she seduces me
and I cannot resist her advances
Under the blanket of stars she gazes at me
and I cannot refuse her glances
Drawn to her darkness
I come in under the belly of her shadow
Entranced by her obscurity
I enter in where knowledge is no more

Here I must stay under the dark gaze of her loving
Here I must rest under the fragrance of her silence
Here I must wait under the shadow of her wooing
while she speaks to me
and she sings to me
and she cradles me
and croons to me
in words no other may utter
in a language unknown to any other lover

And so she will charm me and bind me
She will pierce me and bless me
She will fill me and empty me
She will rouse me and quiet me
She will wound me and heal me
She will quicken me and deaden me
in her deep and unyielding darkness
which no tongue may name nor finger trace
no searching plumb nor mind guess

And I will enter into this darkness
where I have never walked before
And I will submit into this darkness
to a terror never dared before
And I will yield into this darkness
to a loving never ventured before

And of her darkness I must know and I must know nothing
And in this darkness I must be made and I must be unmade
And of her darkness I must be possessed and dispossessed of all
    things

Winter

Where the wood is dry
Where no green things lie
Where the wild things fly
   There am I

Where the stream is still
Where the wind is shrill
Where the ice forms chill
   There am I

Where the ground is hard
Where the earth is scarred
Where the path is barred
   There am I

Where no leaf is seen
Where the year is lean
Where the grief is keen
   There am I

Where the blood runs slow
Where no waters flow
Where the hope is low
   There am I

Where the dark is strong
Where the night is long
Through the winter's song
   There am I

Notes, Sources and Acknowledgements

Chapter 1: Praying Like a Woman

A shorter version of the introduction was published in *The Woman's Christian Yearbook 2003*, edited by Natalie K. Watson, Brigitte Enzer-Probst and Hanna Strack (Norwich, Canterbury Press, 2002).

Chapter 2: Motherless Children Weeping in the World Alone

'Morning sickness': I have never been pregnant; this poem is not intended to be read literally. Rather, I am using the imagery of morning sickness and birth as an analogy for the creative process of bringing to birth, which for me has involved lethargy, sickness and listlessness, as well as the trust that, ultimately, the enduring of such temporary affliction is in the service of life.

'Lament for a lost friendship': this piece uses and reworks the Good Friday reproaches traditionally put in the mouth of God reproaching his people, here used by a woman reproaching the friend who has abandoned her. The piece quotes from Psalm 139.23–4, Psalm 137.5–6, Psalm 123.1–4 and Song of Songs 2.14.

The collect, 'Christ whose piercing gaze . . .' was originally published in *Searching Stories Study Guide* by Nicola Slee (Birmingham, Christian Education, 2002), p. 39. I am grateful to Christian Education for permission to reprint this, and a number of other pieces originally published by them.

The collects 'Absent yet present God' and 'God of all comfort and strength' were originally published in *Songs of Life Study Guide* by Nicola Slee (Birmingham, Christian Education, 2001), pp. 25 and 30.

'Prayer to Mary' appeared in *Remembering Mary Study Guide* by Nicola Slee (Birmingham, Christian Education, 2000), p. 33.

The 'Eucharist for World AIDS Day' was written for World AIDS Day 2003 and used for the first time in the chapel at Queen's, Birmingham.

'Sower' was first published in the Cairns mailing, November 1997. The Aston Training Scheme was founded by the Anglican House of Bishops in 1977 to prepare men and women for ordination. I was Director of Studies from 1992 to 1997, when the scheme was closed.

Chapter 3: Storming the Silence

Marge Piercy's poem, 'A just anger' is to be found in her collection, *Circles on the Water* (New York, Alfred A. Knopf, 1982).

'Speaking of silence: a reproach' originally formed part of *Broken Silence: Women Finding a Voice*, a liturgy for women's voices and congregational participation devised for a study day at Southwark Cathedral in January 1990 (Women in Theology, 1993).

'Women's silence: a confession' also formed part of this liturgy, but was subsequently published as 'Broken silence' in *Celebrating Women: The New Edition*, edited by Hannah Ward, Jennifer Wild and Janet Morley (London, SPCK, 1995), p. 33.

'The fathers': this poem is not directed against fathers *per se*, but uses 'the fathers' as an image for the long line of patriarchs, the ruling fathers in Church and society, both externalized and internalized in women's psyches, who have exercised control over women's minds and bodies for centuries.

'Mary Magdalene: a liturgy of denunciation and reclamation' was prepared for a study day on Mary Magdalene at Methodist Central Hall in July 2000 and subsequently published in *Mary Magdalene: Apostle to the Apostles* (London: Churches Together in Britain and Ireland, 2001). I am grateful to CTBI for permission to reprint. The quotation by Elisabeth Moltmann-Wendel is from *The Women Around Jesus* (London, SCM, 1982), p. 64.

'Texts of terror' takes its title and theme from Phyllis Trible's book of that name.

'Veneration of the cross': I wrote this during one Holy Week while staying at Malling Abbey when I was reading the fierce and shocking feminist critique of classic atonement theology, *Christianity, Patriarchy and Abuse*, edited by Joanne Carlson Brown and Carole R. Bohn (Pilgrim Press, 1989). Reading this book caused a major crisis of faith for me as I wrestled to find some kind of meaning in the events of Holy Week which would not be a glorification of suffering and violence. This struggle was focused in particular around the liturgy of the Veneration of the Cross practised in the community on Good Friday, when a simple wooden cross is passed around the congregation for veneration, and prayers are offered in thanksgiving for the cross.

'Prayer for friends turned enemy' and 'What have we done?' appeared originally in *Prayers for Friends and Enemies* edited by Ruth Burgess (Glasgow, Wild Goose Publications, 2003), p. 41. I am grateful to Wild Goose Publications for their permission to reprint these prayers and several other pieces first published by them in their anthologies.

Chapter 4: Under the Brooding Breast

'Dark', 'Edge', 'Journey', and 'A litany of waiting' appeared in the Cairns mailing at various times between 1997 and 1998.

'Hole': during a period when I was ill with Chronic Fatigue Syndrome, Jo Ind sent me one of the sayings from the Taoist classic, the *Tao Teh Ching*, which spoke to me deeply of the creative significance of emptiness. I wrote this poem in response to saying number 11, which goes as follows:

Thirty spokes converge upon a single hub;
It is on the hole in the center that the use of the cart hinges.

We make a vessel from a lump of clay;
It is the empty space within the vessel that makes it useful.

We make doors and windows for a room;
But it is these empty spaces that make the room livable.

Thus, while the tangible has advantages,
It is the intangible that makes it useful.

(From the *Tao Teh Ching* by Lao Tzu, translated by John C. H. Wu, Boston, Shambhala Publications, 1989).

'Wrestler' appeared in *Celebrating Women: The New Edition*, edited by Hannah Ward, Jennifer Wild and Janet Morley (London, SPCK, 1995), p. 115.

'Prayer for the waiting time' first appeared in the Cairns mailing, June 1998, and subsequently in *Cradle of Life: The Methodist Prayer Handbook 2003 for Methodists in Britain and Ireland*, edited by Maureen Edwards (Peterborough, Methodist Publishing House, 2003), p. 73.

'Laying of the cloth: an Advent prayer' originally formed part of a liturgy for Advent 1998 prepared for the Queen's Foundation, Birmingham, in which the congregation wove a simple cloth and placed it in a cradle in the centre of the church. I am grateful to Helen Cameron for working with me on this liturgy.

'The darkness of God: a blessing' was published in *A Book of Blessings* edited by Ruth Burgess (Glasgow, Wild Goose Publications, 2001), pp. 130–1.

Chapter 5: Dare to Declare

'Conversations with Muse' appeared first in *Celebrating Women: The New Edition*, edited by Hannah Ward, Jennifer Wild and Janet Morley (London, SPCK, 1995), pp. 113–14.

'Nativity' also appeared in *Celebrating Women*, pp. 111–12.

'Open our lips' formed part of the *Broken Silence* liturgy (details above). The second part of this piece draws on Isaiah 6.1–8, Psalm 29.3–9 and Psalm 51.16.

'A single woman's manifesto' appeared in *Courage to Love: An Anthology of Inclusive Worship Material* edited by Geoffrey Duncan (London, DLT, 2002), pp. 10–11. I am grateful to DLT for permission to reprint this piece and a number of others, as listed below.

'With others' first appeared in the Cairns mailing, November 1999.

'Easter creed' appeared in *Women Included: A Book of Services and Prayers* by the St Hilda Community (London, SPCK, 1991), p. 51.

'God of all time' was published in *Songs of Life Study Guide* by Nicola Slee (Birmingham, Christian Education, 2001), p.19.

Chapter 6: Unfreezing the Frame

'A litany of women's voices' formed part of the *Broken Silence* liturgy (as above).

'The prostitute's story' and 'Widow of the disappeared' were first published in *Searching Stories Study Guide* by Nicola Slee (Birmingham, Christian Education, 2002), pp. 27–8, 21 and 32–3.

Chapter 7: This Woman's Body

'Red': I wrote this poem not long before having my hysterectomy. My periods, over an extended time, had gradually been becoming heavier and heavier, due to the fibroids in my uterus. Thus the excessive language of the poem is, in this case, quite literal: the bleeding was, indeed, 'a veritable flood' that could not be staunched.

'Wilgefortis and her sisters': the legend of Wilgefortis tells how this Christian convert took a vow of virginity and, in order to dissuade suitors, prayed to become unattractive to men. As a result, she grew a moustache and a beard. Her father had her crucified; while on the cross she prayed that all who remembered her passion should be liberated from all encumbrances and troubles.

'A summer fruits grace', 'A grace after sickness', 'A grace for eating alone' and 'God bless the backs' first appeared in *Blessed Be Our Table: Graces for Mealtimes and*

Reflections on Food edited by Neil Paynter (Glasgow, Wild Goose Publications, 2003), pp. 280, 261, 66 and 18 respectively.

Chapter 8: So Many Kinds of Awesome Love

'So many kinds of awesome love' appeared in *Courage to Love*, pp. 62–3 (details as above).

'Weaving of the cloth: an Advent canticle' originally formed part of a liturgy for Advent 1998 prepared for the Queen's Foundation, Birmingham, in which the congregation wove a simple cloth and placed it in a cradle in the centre of the church. Each person was given a length of wool or twine, the lengths were tied together to form longer strands and these were then worked into a simple hand loom so that a modest-sized blanket was made during the service, and then placed in the crib.

'Blessing at the table' appeared in *A Book of Blessings*, p. 145 (as above).

'Thanksgiving for friends' appeared in *Prayers for Friends and Enemies*, p. 27 (as above).

'Charis' and 'Making love with you' appeared in *Courage to Love*, pp. 185–6 and 187–8 (as above). 'Charis' is the Greek word for 'grace', used in the New Testament for the undeserved, gratuitous love of God.

The collects 'God of unconditional love' and 'God of the defenceless little ones' appeared in *Searching Stories*, pp. 29 and 34 (as above).

Chapter 9: All Golden Peach

The graces appeared in *Blessed Be Our Table*, pp. 272, 88, 16–17, 19 and 21 (as above).

A version of 'Abbey praise' appeared in *Songs of Life*, p. 41 (as above). The 'name day' of a religious is the anniversary of their profession, when they make a commitment to the religious community and take on their religious name.

The eucharistic prayer was written for the Queen's Foundation for Ecumenical Theological Education, and forms part of the revised Queen's Rite. I am grateful to Paul Collins for inviting me to write a eucharistic prayer (something I had never attempted and would not have attempted without the invitation) and for his critical feedback, as well as that of other colleagues.

Chapter 10: The Edge of God

I am grateful to David Hart for the stimulating metaphor of the 'edge of God' which forms the title of this chapter. The phrase 'bring many names' is the title of one of Brian Wren's superb hymns in his original and provocative study of religious language, *What Language Shall I Borrow?* (SCM, 1989), pp. 143 ff.

'The water, the fire, the body': this poem/prayer is a reflection on and response to the glorious Benjamin Britten memorial window by John Piper in the parish church at Aldeburgh, on the Suffolk coast. The window comprises three lights depicting, respectively, Britten's three Church Operas: *Curlew River*, *The Prodigal Son* and *The Burning, Fiery Furnace*.

'Litany to a dark God' first appeared in the Cairns mailing, and subsequently formed part of a BBC Radio 4 Sunday morning service crafted by Gavin D'Costa and broadcast on Sunday 15 September 2002 from St James Priory, Bristol.

Biblical Index

Note: throughout these indexes, *italic type* indicates titles; roman type indicates first lines.

Liturgical Season and Pastoral Theme Index

Liturgical Genre Index

Index of Titles and First Lines

Index of Titles and First Lines   ◆   151